Overclocked

Surviving the System
That You Built To Survive

Ian P. Gregoire

Overclocked: Surviving The System That You Built To Survive

Cover design by: Ian Gregoire
Publisher: Ian Gregoire
ISBN (Paperback): 979-8-9993175-0-6

ISBN (Hardcover): 979-8-9993175-2-0
ISBN (E-book): 979-8-9993175-1-3
Printed in the United States of America
First Edition

For the teachers, first responders, dispatchers, active-duty military, veterans, healthcare workers, and everyone else filling gaps and holding the line.

You're not alone.

You're not broken.

You're just too good at survival.

Overclocked: Surviving The System That You Built To Survive

How to Read This Book

This book uses computer language to talk about human burnout.

You don't need to understand tech, code, or engineering to get it. If a word feels unfamiliar, just swap it for something more human:

Overclocked = overwhelmed

Firewall = emotional protection

System crash = a shutdown that isn't visible from the outside

Looping = stuck thoughts you can't turn off

Patch = small adjustments that helped you survive

The breach log is how I tracked what broke through my system. Sometimes it's a list of questions I couldn't stop asking. Sometimes it's a moment that forced me to see something I'd buffered for years.

These logs are a diagnostic tool.

The breach is when the voice cracked, the protocol failed, or the emotion finally got through.

I didn't write them to sound poetic. I wrote them because they were the only way I knew I was still running. I didn't choose metaphors to be clever. I used them because emotions aren't logical.

Read at your own pace. Start at the beginning, or flip to whatever chapter you need.

If something resonates, sit with it. If it doesn't, skip it. There's no single "right" way to go through this.

Take what works and leave what doesn't.

If a chapter gets heavy, pause. Put the book down. It's okay if this is not for you.

This wasn't written for everyone.

It was written to give people like me a different way to view the system.

Cause and effect.

That's it.

Come back if you need to.

We are not broken.

We're running a system that's been through more than most people have ever seen.

This is the user manual for a system we never learned to operate.

How to Read This Book

Author's Note

This didn't start as something I thought I would finish. I just knew that something had to give for the sake of my health.

I wanted to feel how I used to, back when I lived like everyone else.

Now I just look forward to going to bed.

It began as a timeline. One specific moment pushed me onto a path I never wanted but couldn't avoid. I started documenting every event that changed me and forced unconscious adaptation. I was hoping clarity might emerge by mapping them out.

I was logging failures in real time, hoping a pattern would appear.

Over the course of the next 96 hours, I started figuring out what was happening.

Something inside me had begun leaking clarity faster than my firewall could suppress it.

The breach was underway. I didn't know it then, but I was already documenting it.

I identified around fifteen life events that installed metaphorical patches into my internal operating system. Each patch changed my behavior, always with protective intent.

It struck me that what I experienced might resonate with someone else, so I started exploring how to share this message.

I wanted people to know I had a name for it. Maybe it would help them name it, too.

It isn't about a diagnosis; it was pattern recognition. I had been unconsciously training for this my whole life.
I was hoping other people had too.

I sent it to a friend of mine to read. A few days later, I got a text message. He described some dark times he had been through.

He told me that someone somewhere needed to see it.

A few days later, another friend sent me a message about nightmares he had been having from a recent emergency response.

This book became urgent. As I started revising, polishing, fixing, and second-guessing, I heard the voice.

It was the voice that helps me make good decisions. I had been hearing that voice for as long as I could remember.

It always said the same things.

Don't bother.

You won't finish.

It'll become another discarded project.

It insisted no one would care and convinced me I was alone and that something was fundamentally wrong with me. That contentment was out of reach.

This book is a "Diagnostic Memoir". A map written in systems language.

I realized that my brain had adapted to experiences over numerous decades, downloading patches that rewrote my internal software.

These patches enhanced my performance, allowing me to function at high levels under stress.

Only now am I beginning to clearly see the severe limitations and hidden costs of operating this way indefinitely.

I wake up tired, go to work tired, and return home emotionally vacant. Despite loved ones, privilege, and comfort, my ability to truly enjoy life has steadily faded, seemingly without explanation. The firewall still exists, but it doesn't function the way it once did. Another system is emerging, something simultaneously new and strangely familiar.

It moves forward carefully and deliberately.

The new system tells me clearly:

The patches are installed.

It's time to reboot.

Table of Contents

Internal Incident Management: Explained

For readers who aren't familiar with computer terms, here's what these words mean in this book:

Operating System (OS) - The basic program that runs your computer. In this book, it means the basic way your mind works, especially the parts built when you were stressed or scared.

Overclocked - When you push a computer harder than it's supposed to go. Here, it means pushing yourself beyond what's healthy.

Firewall - A security system that blocks bad stuff from getting into your computer. In this book, it's the voice in your head that tries to protect you, but sometimes goes too far.

System Crash - When a computer stops working. Here, it means when you shut down emotionally but still look fine on the outside.

Buffering - When a video pauses to load. In this book, it means the pause between feeling something and actually dealing with it.

Legacy Code - Old computer programs that still run even when they're outdated. Here, it means old ways of thinking and acting that you learned when you were young, but don't help you anymore.

Patch - A fix for computer software. In this book, it means making small changes to improve how your mind works.

Firewall Breach - When someone breaks into a computer system. Here, it means when new thoughts break through your mental defenses.

Heat Threshold - The temperature at which a computer starts to break down. In this book, it's the point where you can't handle any more stress.

About Operating Systems: Some of these patterns overlap with neurodivergent traits. This isn't about pathologizing neurological differences or suggesting they need fixing. It's about recognizing when survival adaptations layer on top of natural brain differences, creating systems that serve us.

Until they don't.

A Quick Guide to IFS

If the first section gives you the technical specs, this one's more like emotional architecture.

Internal Family Systems (IFS), developed by Dr. Richard Schwartz, is a psychological model that views the mind as a system of distinct "parts." Each part has its own role, personality, and protective intent. Rather than seeing the mind as a single entity, IFS presents it as a complex system of subpersonalities that interact and influence behavior.

Core Roles in IFS:

Managers: Proactive protectors that try to maintain control and prevent distress by managing our internal and external worlds.

Firefighters: Reactive protectors, activated when Managers fail, stepping in urgently to suppress emotional pain or distract from uncomfortable feelings.

Exiles: Vulnerable parts carrying emotional wounds, traumas, or painful memories. Managers and Firefighters typically try to keep these hidden or suppressed.

Self: The core essence of an individual, characterized by calmness, clarity, compassion, curiosity, creativity, courage, confidence, and connectedness.

How I Found IFS:

I didn't start this journey knowing anything about Internal Family Systems. While writing this manuscript and documenting what felt like a mental firewall breach, I was frantically googling terms to explain why my brain worked the way it did. That's how I stumbled across IFS. Finding it felt like discovering someone had already mapped out a landscape I'd spent my life navigating blindfolded. It gave me clear language to describe the mental systems and protective routines I'd intuitively sensed but couldn't fully articulate.

This book isn't meant as clinical guidance, just an honest reflection of my journey, with a map provided by the invaluable work of Dr. Richard Schwartz and the IFS community.

For further reading, I highly recommend:
Schwartz, R. C. (2019). *Internal family systems therapy* (2nd ed.). Guilford Press

1: Power-On Self-Test

I didn't write this because I figured anything out. I wrote it because I was tired.

The kind that makes you wonder if you're secretly broken, because functionally, you're still performing everything you do at a high level.

I don't have answers. I have logs. Field entries. Diagnostic snapshots. Proof of a system that never got a reboot, just layers of protocol built over years of doing what had to be done.

It was perfectionism, not for appearances, but for survival. Control that is rooted in structure. In the belief that failure would collapse everything.

Recently, I met with a therapist as a last-ditch effort to address my exhaustion. Instead, we began examining my thought patterns. He pointed out that other people are wired the same way.

The therapist asked me something simple: "When you're planning and worrying, whose voice do you hear in your head?"

That question cracked something open. I realized I'd been listening to a voice that wasn't even mine.

The breach had begun.

At that moment, I felt like someone had handed me the source code for my nervous system. I started organizing. Listing symptoms like logs. Mapping behaviors like heat signatures.

How long has this been running without anyone noticing?

What I was starting to realize was that my system was designed to translate fear into output while using logic as a buffer against risky emotional exposure, sometimes leaving me frozen mid-sentence or holding tension until I could smile again.

That's the trap with our operating system. At work, it probably looks like discipline or leadership. Everyone leans on you because they know you won't flinch.

You produce at levels far above average. Meanwhile, inside, you're overheating, trying to prevent visible system failure.

You don't need the clinical terms for this to be real. If you did, I'm not qualified to give them to you. If rest feels dangerous or calm reads like a prelude to chaos, you already know the architecture.

It's a fully operational subroutine that shuts you down before anyone else can.

That's what I was running.

This book started as a timeline, with each entry representing a system update. I wanted to reverse-engineer it because I didn't know how else to keep going. It became a last-ditch system dump: an internal black box cracked open before the core was gone forever.

For the first time, I started to wonder if anyone else was quietly debugging their life the same way, writing logs into the dark, trying to stay ahead of a shutdown.

I drafted a LinkedIn post in my head. Unlike most social media, this wasn't a "Look at me! Look at me!" moment; it was meant to test the signal.

To see if anyone else had ever felt this way.

Optimized to the point of exhaustion, useful to the point of disappearance.

Just a line or two on the internet.

"Does anyone else feel like they've been running crisis architecture inside their personality since childhood?"

The voice showed up before I could finish the thought.

No one cares what you think.

Why are you making everything about you?

Other people have more stress than you; get over it.

Don't show them how much you care.

I never posted it.

That voice has always been there; I'm not certain about when it showed up. It mimics logic and sounds like risk management.

It's just shame in BDUs (Battle Dress Utilities), a uniform for Internal Incident Management.

Here's what I didn't realize until I wrote it down: that first voice, the logical one, the strategist? I thought that was me.

I trusted it completely, letting it analyze every room before I entered. It was calm, calculated, and controlled.

It wasn't me, and it wasn't my voice. It was the firewall, software that had been installed years ago, to help me survive.

Somewhere inside that log, something else showed up. It wasn't loud. It didn't offer comfort or yell, "Stay hard, bro."

It whispered:

You've got this.

Fuck that other guy.

He's not protecting you.

He's just keeping them from seeing who you are.

The second voice was mine. I knew what contempt sounds like. That voice wasn't soothing. It was furious, and the anger was precisely controlled.

That voice knew I had been mistaking survival for identity.

It was mad that I had shrunk into something efficient. That I waited this long to start asking questions.

That was the system breach, not collapse or a breakthrough. Just a new voice showing up in the logs.

That's when this shifted from a project to a necessity.

The new voice was taking control.

You are never going to feel worthy, but you're going to do it anyway. That's who you are.

I didn't write this to be understood. I wrote it because I think it's the first step to installing updates.

When I finally went to therapy, it wasn't because I wanted a hug or needed to talk about feelings. It was because I was too tired to keep pretending I wasn't tired.

I had been hearing the firewall's voice in my head for so long...
I'd forgotten what I sounded like.

This is me, remembering.

2: Internal Incident Management

BREACH LOG: [EMOTIONAL BUFFERING DETECTED]

When did emotion become something to suppress instead of something to use?

Why does high performance feel safer than being seen?

When did alcohol become the only reliable shutdown command?

Am I processing life... or just parsing data?

POST-INCIDENT ANALYSIS

Every system has an operator; mine wasn't built for joy; it was built for performance and uptime.

Imagine an emergency response team, an Incident Management Team. A group of police, firefighters, EMS, public works, and emergency management personnel who help stabilize a crisis.

When a crisis hits, their job is clear: respond to the hazard by making the bad thing go away and start recovery by laying the framework for the rebuilding of the community.

Your mind has a similar team, but instead of physical emergencies, like a hurricane or tornado, it handles emotional ones. You learn to manage feelings such as sadness, anger, or anxiety by mitigating those internal hazards. Rather than fully experiencing emotions, your internal system treats them as incidents to quietly contain.

This allows you to appear calm and functional on the outside.

Initially, this seems helpful because it keeps you calm under pressure. The hidden cost is suppressing emotions while preventing genuine processing. This can leave you emotionally numb and exhausted beneath your surface composure.

This internal Incident Management Team is always alert and ready to respond. In the background, it quietly drains your emotional resources, leading to burnout disguised as stability.

Internal Incident Management is the unconscious operating system you install to handle life's chaos, uncertainty, and pressure. It's not just about managing emotions or reacting to problems; it's about continuously scanning, forecasting, and stabilizing your mental and emotional environment.

Over time, this system quietly takes control, running in the background. Eventually, you mistake it for your own personality.

It's not managing negative emotion; it's micromanaging all emotion. Eventually, nothing can get through.

It turns vigilance into autopilot, precision into rigidity, and emotional buffering into standard procedure.

Ultimately, the very thing that once made you feel safe becomes the invisible barrier preventing you from fully experiencing your own life.

The update was downloaded without conscious installation: if the environment cannot be controlled, the emotional response must be controlled.

Boot camp wasn't a test of strength.

It was a test of invisibility.

The Recruit Division Commanders made that clear early. You didn't want to be noticed. Excellence wasn't rewarded; it was punished. The best recruits were cycled periodically. These were PT cycles that went beyond training into punishment.

Exercise as a weapon.

You do burpees until you vomit, then you clean it up and do more burpees. The cycle breaks your will, not just your body. Even the best recruits were cycled to remind everyone that no one was safe from scrutiny.

I learned that standing out was dangerous.

Recruits who cried, showed anger, or displayed fear were punished. I learned invisibility.

The safest place was the gray area, just enough effort to avoid punishment but never enough to draw attention. The "gray man" mindset became my first leadership lesson: maintain control without inviting inspection.

The days were physically brutal and mentally relentless.

The Navy didn't teach emotional regulation; it taught shutdown.

Alcohol became the only reliable cooling system. I didn't drink on duty, but I started the moment I left work.

It signaled my brain to stand down. It silenced the scanner, softened alerts, and muted the critic.

It reliably signaled my brain to go silent.

It felt efficient, not dangerous. That was precisely the point.

I began needing that silence, not out of addiction, but as a break from relentless analysis.

No one celebrated it, and no one stopped it.

AFTER-ACTION REVIEW

What job taught you to perform painlessly and did anyone notice you weren't okay?

What did you first use to power down that started as relief but became routine?

Can you recall a time when silence was celebrated, not questioned?

CORRECTIVE ACTIONS

Send a short message to someone who assumes you're always steady.

Say: "Carrying a lot today. Not a crisis, just FYI."

Let that be enough. No status report. No justification.

3: Control Interface

BREACH LOG: [CONTROL LOOP INITIATED]

When did leadership become silent over-functioning?

Why does letting someone help feel like a liability?

Why does capability keep expanding until it breaks you?

Can you lead without disappearing?

What's the cost of always being in control?

POST-INCIDENT ANALYSIS

The firewall I'd built wasn't serving me anymore. It had become a force that dampened everything, funneling my energy exclusively into strategic and tactical calculations, leaving little room for anything else.

The first wave was helplessness, quickly followed by fury. How had I let myself get here?

Reflecting, I recognized that I'd blamed myself. Anything within my control or influence that didn't go perfectly felt like personal failure. My logic insisted failures came from insufficient planning or overlooked contingencies.

A pivotal experience came in 2009 at a "Seven Habits of Highly Effective People" class. Beginning to understand the circles of control, influence, and concern resonated deeply.

The smallest, innermost circle holds the things you can directly change: your actions, choices, even your attitude.

The middle circle represents what you can affect indirectly, through influence. Things like helping a subordinate learn by being a good example or having a difficult conversation with coworkers.

The outer circle is everything you care about but can't really change on your own, from global events to other people's decisions.

Focusing on that outer ring wastes energy and leads to frustration. By concentrating on what you control and where you can influence, you make real progress and build credibility.

There's a catch: as you prove your competence, more responsibilities get piled onto your control circle until it's so crowded you start to feel overwhelmed all over again.

By keeping your circles balanced, you stay productive and avoid burning out.

I'd been wasting energy on things I couldn't change and resolved to redirect more efficiently. Yet, as my capability grew, responsibilities expanded endlessly.

Each successful influence mission became another task completed, reinforcing the idea that a working method should be repeated indefinitely.

Eventually, everything became an influence mission.

My reframe became bluntly practical, inspired by a line from Bunk from the show "The Wire":

"Stop giving a fuck when it's not your turn to give a fuck."

It felt like this was aimed directly at me, but living by it was far harder than agreeing with it.

A test arrived later on, when my daughter offered to mow the lawn because I was sick. Accepting her help marked a tangible step toward breaking the cycle. Watching her mow, anxiety and guilt surged. I thought she shouldn't do this alone.

I worried about her safety and the neighbor's judgments while I rested inside.

I forced myself to challenge those feelings. She had genuinely volunteered to support me. It struck me that I'd been consistently denying support, unintentionally isolating myself from those closest to me.

My world had split in two: what I was responsible for, and everyone else, including my family. Those spheres almost never overlapped.

Watching my daughter finish mowing did little initially to make me feel better. The fears of injury or judgment. I'd rather mow the lawn sick than imagine her hurt. Alongside this protective instinct, I realized these tasks were critical steps in building her confidence and independence.

My anxiety wasn't just a typical worry. It was a fiercely protective instinct rooted deep in my past. I'm not certain where this instinct began, but I recall vividly a high school fight in which I had given a fuck when it wasn't my turn to give a fuck. I jumped into a situation to protect someone else. This memory, detailed later, symbolized my lifelong habit of placing others above myself.

Today, my dominant feeling is exhaustion mixed with clarity.

It feels like it should be pride or regret.

I'm finally starting to untangle decades of protective instincts, seeing them as powerful forces that, unchecked, leave me emotionally depleted.

The breach opened pathways to reconnection and integration, beginning with allowing others to step in and support me.

I had been available everywhere except the place that mattered:

Home.

AFTER-ACTION REVIEW

What tasks do you take on that no one asked you to own?

When was the last time accepting help made you more, not less?

Where has responsibility become a substitute for connection?

CORRECTIVE ACTIONS

Let someone complete a task you normally take over.

Say thank you. Not "I'll fix it later."

Let the discomfort sit.

It's not about quality.

It's about recovery.

4: Early Warning System

BREACH LOG: [EMOTIONAL RADAR ACTIVATED]

When did you start reading tone faster than words?

How early did you feel responsible for someone else's emotions?

Are you protecting yourself, or managing everyone around you?

Is your empathy strategic or sincere?

POST-INCIDENT ANALYSIS

My internal operating system began downloading an update subconsciously. If I couldn't control my environment, it would consume me. I didn't feel stronger; I felt colder, safer.

When I got out of the Navy in 2001, I started a job as a police and fire dispatcher, and something changed. Erikk came into the dispatch center about eighteen months after I did. He was fast, sharp, sarcastic, and field-seasoned. We bonded immediately.

He became my shadow. We synced across shifts, radios, and instinct. For a while, he was my best friend. He wasn't the kind of friend you planned vacations with, but the kind of friend who understood your silence.

Over time, I watched him fray. His drinking grew darker. The edge in his humor wasn't tactical anymore; it was tired, and he was depressed. I made the decision to step back; looking back, it was more of a calculation. I cared about him; he was my brother, but I didn't know how to stay close without becoming the next casualty.

Years later, when we reconnected, it felt like nothing had changed. But under the surface, everything had.

In that same window, I found unexpected mentorship: Tammy, Jackie, and Lauren. They were my supervisors, dispatchers who led not through formulas, but through presence.

Especially Tammy.

Tammy didn't lead by command. She led like a force of nature. Sharp. Dry. Maternal but still a hardass when needed. She wasn't everyone's favorite but everyone respected her effectiveness.

She was the first person I watched lead without asking for permission. She didn't need to control everything. She knew where to apply pressure and when to leave room.

Looking back, I think she was running her own system. Calculating in real time how every word would ripple across the dispatch center, not to dominate, but to protect.

It was the first time I saw what leadership looked like without posturing and ego.

I didn't know how to be like that.

Not yet.

Ignoring emotions doesn't erase them. They build pressure, like steam in a closed system.

Using terms I understand, I began calling it Internal Incident Management. Becoming so adept at managing emotional responses that genuine feelings vanish, replaced by data processed rather than experiences lived.

From the outside, it looks stable. From the inside, it feels disconnected from life.

If Internal Incident Management is the system that governs emotional suppression, the firewall is the first responder, trained not to feel, but to eliminate hazards.

A firewall is like a security guard or a bouncer for your computer or network. It stands between your device and the internet, checking everything that tries to get in or out.

If something looks safe, the firewall lets it through; if it seems dangerous or sketchy, it blocks it. It's basically a digital gatekeeper that helps keep bad stuff like viruses, hackers, or unwanted connections from sneaking onto your system.

When I was around five or six, I had a babysitter named Ann. She tried to put me down for a nap one afternoon, but I wasn't having it. Determined and defiant, I decided to sneak out and visit a friend who lived two streets over. Without telling Ann, I slipped outside and walked along the edge of a busy road, "Grizzly," my loyal German Shepherd, herding me protectively, keeping me safely off the pavement.

When I finally arrived at my friend's house, her parents were shocked and immediately called my mother. They promptly took me home.

As soon as I walked through the door, I saw Ann. She was visibly upset. What struck me most deeply was her guilt. She even apologized to me, which confused me at the time. She hadn't done anything wrong; it was my choice to leave.

Even at that young age, I understood I was responsible for the pain and fear on her face. I didn't grasp the full implications then, but looking back, my actions could have cost Ann her job.

That incident is one of my earliest vivid memories, and I think it's when my emotional radar first switched on.

I became intensely aware of my impact on other people's emotional states. It wasn't long before this awareness began to shape my behavior at home. Even when I was small, I liked order.

Things always had to make sense. I hated it when things were unfair, inefficient, or done sloppily just because. I was also deeply reactive, especially to tone.

You could scream in my face, and I'd be fine. But a slight shift in vocal pitch or an unexpected pause would have me analyzing the conversation for days.

I thought this was my personality. Now I know it was my brain learning to read danger in people's voices. I was building an early warning system without even knowing it.

Like most kids, when I was in third grade, I was fascinated with dinosaurs. We visited the natural history museum in D.C. frequently; it was the first time I noticed that people lived on the street.

I questioned my mom about it. I didn't understand the concept of homelessness at all. My mom did her best to explain it, but it had an overwhelming impact on my psyche. I thought about it for weeks.

In Mrs. Martin's class, we had to write a third-grade version of an essay. I remember being excited about the smaller green lines on the grey paper.

I wrote about my experience in D.C. I don't remember what I wrote exactly, but I remember the reaction. Mrs. Martin called my mom after sending it home with a star. She wanted my mom to know that most kids don't have the ability to interpret emotional impact into words at that age.

I bet my mother still has that paper; she keeps things like that.

In fifth grade, there was a kid named Ryan who everyone knew as a bully. He thrived on intimidation, taunting classmates in the hallway or playground, pushing until someone snapped back, feeding into exactly what he seemed to want: conflict.

For some reason, my internal radar saw through it clearly. I sensed something else behind his 10-year-old bravado: loneliness. I noticed tiny hesitations in his movements, a subtle pause before each insult. It was like he was following a script rather than truly wanting to fight. One day, as he approached, ready to deliver his usual dose of hallway intimidation, I beat him to it, instinctively blurting out, "Hey Ryan, those shoes look new. Where'd you get them?"

He froze, utterly disoriented. The tough mask he usually wore slipped, just for a second, replaced by genuine confusion. "Uh, Foot Locker," he muttered, glancing away nervously.

It was enough.

The encounter ended before it began. Each time after, whenever I saw Ryan gearing up to provoke someone, me included, I'd intercept with simple, disarming questions: "What'd you do this weekend?" or "Did you catch the game last night?" Each interruption felt instinctual and spontaneous, rather than planned, but always effective.

Over time, our dynamics transformed entirely. He didn't become my friend exactly, but he stopped targeting me. It was as if my unplanned questions disrupted the rhythm he relied on, stripping away the fuel that drove his aggression. Without ever consciously choosing it, I'd found a strategy born purely from instinctual awareness, reshaping an interaction before it could escalate into conflict.

Years later, I'd recognize this moment as a clear demonstration of an operating system that was already scanning for threats and recalibrating social dynamics, long before I understood that was even a skill I had developed.

The divorce wasn't quiet, and it rewrote everything.

There was no single villain in the divorce, and no clean way to narrate how I interpreted the experience. What I can say is this: my internal compass didn't break. It recalibrated. I lost a family structure. With that, I lost clarity on who I was supposed to be. Not in a scorched-earth kind of way. More like a slow drift from the center. From right and wrong to safe or dangerous. From fair and unfair to effective or not.

My mother was single then, and I could clearly see the exhaustion on her face when she came home after work from her second job.

Recognizing this, I proactively started doing yard work and keeping the house clean to alleviate her burden. It brought me deep satisfaction to watch her walk in and simply go to bed without having to clean or organize.

That moment of relief on her face was worth the effort.

Beneath the satisfaction lay a growing anxiety, a persistent feeling I couldn't quite articulate as a child. It felt as though I was a cartoon character desperately plugging leaks in a dam with my fingers, holding back a flood. This constant vigilance started affecting my social interactions as well.

I began to adopt a caretaker role no one had asked for.

Like most kids in survival mode, I adapted: coding under load, not assigning fault. I learned which version of myself earned praise and which earned punishment. I started tracking tone shifts, facial expressions, and body language long before I had words for it. I became fluent in the unsaid.

I believe this is what accelerated the development of my emotional intelligence. I didn't always know that term. When I was actively trying to use it, I called it my radar. It wasn't wisdom as I had thought, but it was self-defense.

At school, I kept adjusting. One version with teachers, another on the bus, another after school. Not manipulation, it was insurance against getting hurt.

These survival adaptations look different depending on who you are. Some disappear into competence and control. Some become hyper-responsible caretakers who can't say no. The wiring varies, but the cost is similar: trading authenticity for safety, presence for performance.

Middle school was a reset: new building, new code of survival. It was 1991. No internet. No cell phones. It was body language, bus routes, and fast emotional calculus.

I was one of the only white kids in my class. I wasn't bullied. I wasn't excluded, but I was different. The rhythm was different. Speech, posture, timing, volume. There was a language in the room, and I didn't speak it.

I learned it, not as a performance, but as a survival instinct.

My experience isn't what people of color endure while code-switching under systemic harm. I was adapting to a culture I didn't grow up in, not facing institutional exclusion. But that adaptation accelerated everything.

I didn't want to be liked. I wanted to blend. To be quiet enough not to draw heat, confident enough not to draw pity.

I matched cadence and calibrated posture. I laughed on beat, not too early, not too loud. I watched people watching me. It wasn't a conscious strategy or social grace.

This was pattern recognition under pressure.

I was perfecting threat management, the only way a sixth grader knows how.

It became my default operating mode, and I never noticed it happening.

AFTER-ACTION REVIEW

When did emotional awareness shift from connection to control?

Were you reading the room to support people, or to stay safe in it?

Can you trace that back to a face, a tone, a silence that taught you early vigilance?

Is your emotional radar a strength... or a symptom?

CORRECTIVE ACTIONS

Track your next moment of "emotional scanning.

Let your system observe without immediately adapting.

Note the tension that follows. That's data.

When you next notice someone in distress, resist the urge to manage it.

Say, "That sounds hard," and stop. No solving. No fixing.

Let your presence do what your system never trusted it could.

5: Security Settings

BREACH LOG: [FIREWALL INSTALLATION COMPLETE]

When did preparation replace presence?

Why does fitting in require emotional camouflage?

How often do you monitor the room instead of showing up in it?

When did safety mean vanishing?

POST-INCIDENT ANALYSIS

I still do it.

I don't mean to, but I can adjust to almost any room and any group. It looks like a social skill. It reads like leadership.

Underneath?

It's code-switching that never powers down, a system always reading people to decide who I'm allowed to be.

Fluency isn't the same as belonging. It's performance stability.

Sometimes, I don't know if I'm connecting or preventing collapse.

That's not charisma.

That's legacy code: old programming that your brain wrote during hard times. It still runs, even if it doesn't help anymore.

Legacy code is inherited under pressure. It's code that worked well for you at one time.

When it did work, it was in a different environment and under different threats. Now it introduces friction or instability because the system has changed, and the code hasn't.

Legacy code is the version of you that got applause when you were hurting.

The performance that passed for strength.
The sarcasm that passed for confidence.
The silence that got mistaken for maturity.

It's the version of you that stepped up before you were ready, and no one ever told you to step down.

Legacy code doesn't break the system; it is the system.

Every day when you wake up, the code is optimizing your day based on yesterday's threats.

You don't delete it because it's bad.
You identify it, so you stop assuming it's the best option.
Most of your current habits, reflexes, and leadership patterns?
They're patches on top of legacy code.

If you've ever thought, *"Why do I act like this even when I know better?"*
That's legacy code running behind the interface.
And the scariest part?
Legacy code *looks like personality.*
But it's not who you are.
It's who you had to be to survive.

It was high school. A guy we called Darrin had become part of our crew. We gave him access to people, to the social currency of being adjacent to the right group.

He was weird. He tried too hard. I still remember his peroxide orange hair, wearing a Green Day T-shirt, and corduroys. I remember asking the friend who introduced us, "Is this for real?"

One day, Darrin picked a fight with someone way out of his weight class, someone who was actually "about that life." Classic high school stupidity, set it up like a movie scene. After school.

Pre-designated time and location.

It was stupid then, and it is stupid now.

Darrin showed up at my house before it happened and asked me to come with him. Not to fight. To make sure he didn't get jumped. He wasn't my favorite person, but it felt like an obligation.

I went.

On the drive over, others saw my car and followed. They didn't really care about Darrin; they were going because they were bored.

In a surprise to absolutely no one, Darrin got his ass kicked. The guy he was fighting, Nick, was on top of him.

Then I saw it: Nick reached into his waistband. I knew Nick must have had a knife.

I didn't know the phrase "bias for action" yet; it was an involuntary reaction. That term wouldn't show up in my vocabulary for another fifteen years.

The protocol was already in place.

I didn't hesitate.

I kicked him in the head.

Hard.

Then again.

I kept kicking until Darrin could get out from under him. We fled.

Later that night, my dad, a retired cop, heard my name come over the scanner. The Police Department wanted to question me.

I remember sitting inside my house that night, looking out the window. Watching the police car sitting outside my house. I wondered if I should go out to talk to them about what had happened.

Dad said no, he would schedule a time to go talk to them on our own. In hindsight, good advice.

We went to the police station the next day, and I explained the situation. The police told me that Nick had a gun. They didn't find it until he was in an ambulance. It was tucked deep in the waistband.

The police never charged me with anything; they understood what had happened. They also told me that Nick was such an asshole that they "unofficially" stopped caring.

The school still cared. It didn't happen on campus, but that didn't matter. Darrin told them it was all my idea. That I had planned it, and that I had escalated it. That I was the aggressor.

I got expelled during my junior year. Darrin got a gold star and a hug from the guidance counselor (that part I made up). The point is, Darrin still graduated and wasn't expelled.

Darrin began turning my friends against me, telling the same story he had told at school.

The lawyer told me not to say anything. Don't talk to the school or Darrin. There is still an ongoing police investigation, and he was going to handle it. Don't try to explain.

A month later, I enlisted in the Navy. Not for control, patriotism, or structure. I had realized: if I didn't build my own system, I'd always be at the mercy of someone else's collapse.

The system I built in childhood was for survival.
This was the interface.
Some kids act out. Others implode. I optimized.

I wasn't the hardest worker, but I was usually the quickest in the room. I processed chaos and delivered answers before people finished asking the question. I became known for wit, sarcasm, and clarity.
I was preempting criticism.

Make them laugh, and you control the tempo. Speak with certainty, and people stop asking questions.

It's a trap.
When everyone sees you as competent, they stop checking on you. They stop offering help. Eventually, you stop expecting it.

You stop seeing relationships as support and start seeing them as a responsibility.

Your Operating System starts to feel like a feature, not a flaw. Order, clarity, and rules reduce variables. They shrink risk.

So, I built systems. First, informal ones. Ways to avoid chaos. To finish before someone changed the rules. To outpace drama by beating the deadline.

Teachers, bosses, peers, they all loved it. They praised the maturity, initiative, and reliability.

Every one of those traits came from vigilance.

I built systems and processes because it was the only way I knew how to reduce risk.

I didn't trust luck or fairness. I trusted fallbacks, exit plans, and contingencies.

I had begun to realize that if you don't design the system, you are the system, subject to every glitch and demand.

That's what I was trying to out-engineer.

That's what the Operating System protected me from.

People started confusing coping mechanisms for personality.

When people called me a natural leader, I felt pressure.
When I get compliments, I get uncomfortable.
Now I had to keep delivering, and the system kept adapting, becoming more complex.
I didn't realize it was protecting me from everything, including connection.

High-functioning isn't healing, it's hiding in plain sight.

At some point, people stop asking if you're okay and start expecting you to make them okay.
This is how the internal erosion starts.
I kept setting personal records and calling them warmups.
Reliability becomes identity, and support creates assumptions.

Every time I showed up under pressure, my expectations for my performance didn't rise; they vanished.

If you complain or point it out, they tell you how great you are and that you are the only one who could pull this off.
They don't realize that's the problem.

You're good at it because you've been running a self-correcting system since you were nine years old, never believing another option existed.

The firewall isn't protective anymore.

It's a prison made of competence.
You're not broken, and you haven't failed.
You're overdue for an update.

You've been so successful that the security settings that got you there became your baseline.

AFTER-ACTION REVIEW

What social skill was actually self-protection?

When have you confused respect with fear of exposure?

Who first taught you to stay unreadable, to stay safe?

CORRECTIVE ACTIONS

Stand in one conversation this week without scanning for risk.

No mirroring. No scripting.

Let the version of you that's off-duty show up and track what happens.

6: Overclocked

BREACH LOG: [PERFORMANCE EXCEEDING SUSTAINABLE THRESHOLD]

Maximize efficiency.

Push the processor. Optimize performance.

Why does slowing down feel more dangerous than staying exhausted?

How close can I get to crashing before anyone notices?

Why do I rehearse conversations in my head, even while brushing my teeth?

When did anxiety start masquerading as discipline?

My son drew a picture of me for Father's Day. It doesn't even look like me. A box with a head and arms? Why were the arms different colors?

What if the system I built to protect me is what's keeping me from connection?

POST-INCIDENT ANALYSIS

The first clear memory I have of being overclocked was early in my emergency management career, around 2009, during the height of the housing market crash. Budget cuts were everywhere, and my project was at serious risk of being eliminated.

To prove my worth, I went into overdrive. Waking up at 3 AM on weekends, updating policies meticulously, managing complex IT projects, and striving relentlessly to demonstrate my value. At the time, I didn't recognize the toll this was taking; in fact, people around me praised my motivation and dedication, which masked internal strain.

In computing, overclocking means pushing a processor beyond factory settings to boost performance, creating more heat and pressure than it was designed for. But there's a trade-off: heat. Overclocked systems run hot. They generate more internal pressure than they were designed to handle.To keep them from crashing, you need a specialized cooling system, constant monitoring, and a willingness to trade long-term durability for short-term output.

When it works, it's brilliant.

When it fails, it's catastrophic.

This chapter is about the moment overclocking shifts from competitive edge to the brink of collapse. We ignore the internal warnings because slowing down feels more dangerous than staying exhausted.

For people like me, being "high-functioning" often means being overclocked. You look successful from the outside. You meet your deadlines, you solve problems, you show up when people need you. In reality, your system is running way too hot.

There were subtle indicators I had missed. My sleep patterns shifted dramatically. I used to be able to lie in bed comfortably, but now my mind would switch gears immediately upon waking, propelling me out of bed, urgently needing to engage in some form of productivity.

My early mornings developed a strict routine: coffee to fuel the engine, an hour of video games for temporary relief, several hours of work, necessary chores, and errands. Then I would dive back into polishing work products. Among these activities, video games became my most significant relief, a distraction to shut down the persistent internal noise.

That noise was relentless, continuous analysis. I would endlessly rehearse and roleplay various potential outcomes to optimize my interactions. Although these rehearsals increased my anxiety, they often led to successful outcomes. This reinforced my belief that I was learning faster than my challenges could keep pace.

This created a reinforcing feedback loop where anxiety and success intertwined tightly, pushing me further into overclocking mode.

The tricky part is that people praise you for it. They say things like "You're so reliable" or "I don't know how you do it all." What they don't see is that you're not doing it all because you're naturally good at it. You're doing it because stopping seems dangerous.

Praise has always made me uncomfortable; I don't like awards or recognition. I never understood why. I now understand that it was piling on additional performance pressure. It was recalibrating my expectations for myself.

Rest doesn't feel like recovery.

When the system slows down, everything you have buffered starts rising to the surface: unfinished thoughts, unresolved mistakes, conversations you've prewritten but never had.

Stillness creates bandwidth for doubt.

You can't sit still because stillness feels like you've abandoned the controls. You stay busy because silence starts asking questions you've worked hard to avoid answering. You don't realize you're trying to drown out noise that's been there your whole life.

When your internal system is built for crisis, rest feels like you're dropping your guard. Stillness feels like you're missing something important.

You rehearse and simulate every conversation like it's a crisis. You rehearse every scenario and have courses of action selected.

So, you keep running more programs, taking on more responsibilities, and solving more problems. Not because you love it, but because slowing down triggers every warning system in your brain.

The exhaustion doesn't hit you all at once. It builds up slowly.

First, you stop enjoying things you used to love. Then you start feeling irritated by small things. Your patience gets shorter. Your body starts sending signals: headaches, a tight jaw, grinding teeth, and trouble sleeping.

You ignore the signals. Things still have to get done. Failure isn't optional. There are systems to maintain. I was managing other people's emotional deficits. Keeping the team steady by anticipating conflict. Rewriting documents at midnight because the phrasing didn't meet my standards.

I was already awake, why not just take care of it and stop thinking about it?

I'll take care of it.

I'm the only one I trust with this.

This feedback loop continued unchecked until recently. My son is four and a half years old. I love him deeply; he's my entire world, but lately, I've struggled to genuinely connect and engage with him.

During a simple moment, he wanted to play "The Floor Is Lava" with his toy dinosaurs, but my mind was elsewhere, weighing this moment against all the tasks still waiting for me.

The immediate emotion I felt was guilt, which subsequently intensified my anxiety, becoming a crucial factor that ultimately led to the emotional breach I experienced later.

Is this the version of me I want to show him?

I kept thinking about that Father's Day drawing. It was box-shaped and miscolored. My son captured me better than I was willing to admit; it was a great effort for a 4-year-old.

He was giving me a moment.

I gave him a pat on the head and put it on the fridge.

It should've been as important to me as it was to him.

The system is going to fail. It's a matter of you noticing when it happens.

AFTER-ACTION REVIEW

What do you consider "rest," and is it truly restful?

When was the last time you completed something and felt satisfied instead of suspicious?

What do you use to justify overclocking, and who taught you that rest means laziness?

Can you name a time that your body tried to get your attention before your brain listened?

CORRECTIVE ACTIONS

Choose one task that you're only doing today to avoid stillness.

Postpone it.

Let your nervous system experience the absence of urgency.

7: Red Team Operations

BREACH LOG: [SIMULATION OVERLOAD DETECTED]

Why am I simulating every possible failure before it even happens?

When did life become something I rehearse, not experience?

Why do I rerun conversations that never went wrong in the first place?

Can I trust growth if it hasn't been pre-vetted by my internal Red Team?

Why does every decision route through threat analysis?

Don't trust. Don't reveal. Don't need. Don't miss anything.

Stop.

You're not protecting anything anymore.

You're just hiding. From yourself. From them.

Stop rehearsing disasters and start living.

POST-INCIDENT ANALYSIS

We were deployed to a small town after a major hurricane.

The town had been leveled.

The mayor and town manager were missing in action, so our Incident Management Team was assigned to gather information and prepare a plan for residential reentry to the area. We got there at 5 PM, and we were told there'd be a meeting with the mayor at 9 AM; he wanted a plan. We were told he wanted options and that he would listen.

We had no information, so we made plans for all contingencies.

I had the team split into three groups and create independent courses of action. We analyzed each one. We scored them and prepped them like lives depended on the outcome, because they did.

When the mayor arrived, he didn't want options. He didn't want logic. He wanted the gates open. Now.

No damage assessment.

No safety rails.

No problem solving.

We didn't fight with him over it; that's not our job. We kept planning for different scenarios. His way, and the right way. We used the illusion of compliance to buy time, while we used local politics to influence the outcome. We were outmaneuvering insanity. Sometimes, the system you serve is the threat.

Our job became engineering the illusion of agreement while doing what's right under the surface. We weren't saving the day. We were doing the right thing because the people in charge weren't doing it.

This was my Red Team focused externally. It looks for weaknesses in a plan and tests vulnerabilities.

In emergency management planning, the Red Team focuses on your plans and procedures. They challenge assumptions, come up with scenarios nobody expects, and push plans until something breaks. They role-play hazards or bad people. It's like doing a hard practice run to make sure your team and your plans are solid before a real disaster hits.

If the firewall protects you from external threats, the Red Team is the subsystem trying to simulate every future failure before it happens.

When you grow up learning that mistakes can be dangerous, your brain develops what I call an internal Red Team. It's like having a critic in your head whose job is to find everything that could go wrong before it does.

This sounds useful, and sometimes it is. But the problem is that your Red Team never takes a break. It's always scanning, always analyzing, always preparing for disaster.

The worst part is that your Red Team doesn't just plan for the upcoming conflict. It plans for recovery from the conflict.

You're not only imagining what could go wrong, you're rehearsing how you'll handle it when it does go wrong.

How you'll bounce back from that, and how you'll explain yourself to everyone.
You've done it a million times. You do it to control the narrative, not build resilience.

Here's how it works: You have a simple task, like sending an email. Your Red Team starts running scenarios. What if they misunderstand what you meant? What if you sounded too casual? What if you sounded too formal? What if there's a typo? You rewrite the email. Then you rewrite it again. You read it five times, checking for anything that could be misinterpreted. A three-sentence message becomes a 10-minute distraction.

By the time you hit send, it's a cross between a hostage negotiation and a TED Talk.

This feels like being thorough. It feels like being responsible. It's actually your brain trying to control outcomes that aren't within your control.

Anytime I need to talk to my kids about breaking long-standing rules (too often), my mind instantly shifts into overdrive. I spend days quietly rehearsing the conversation, scripting each sentence, trying to anticipate every possible reaction.

Recently, my daughter deliberately broke a family rule we'd established years ago. As soon as I realized I had to address it, my brain started running nonstop simulations. I prepared extensively because I expected resistance. More specifically, I anticipated gaslighting because that's often how teenagers (especially mine) defend themselves: by making you question your sanity.

I practiced exactly what I'd say and how I'd react when she inevitably pushed back or tried to deflect. I mapped out counters to her anticipated arguments and excuses, convinced I'd have to hold firm under pressure.

Preparing my defense for interactions with a teenager.
"I don't know what you're talking about."
"Oh, that, I thought you meant something else, well, I didn't do it!"
"Well, maybe I did it, but I didn't mean to do it."
"I didn't mean to do it, so it's not my fault."

I had rehearsed all of it.

Yet, the tension vanished in 5 minutes.

There was no pushback, gaslighting, or elaborate defenses. She simply acknowledged what she'd done, explained why, and accepted responsibility. In a few calm minutes, the tension from the scenarios I'd spent days mentally rehearsing disappeared.

Afterward, I was drained. I'd exhausted myself preparing for a confrontation that never happened. I had been emotionally preparing for a fistfight and ended up with a group hug. My Red Team, designed to avoid failure at all costs, created unnecessary emotional stress by predicting a crisis that existed only in my head.

Your Red Team isn't active because you're weak.
Your Red Team is a superpower.

It's the reason you appear so effective and prepared, even when you're not up to your own standards. It's simulating every possible failure before anyone else even sees the risk. You're running the same vulnerability assessment in your head, 24/7.

How many simultaneous scenario branches am I currently running?

Email response strategies, family budget, social dynamics for tomorrow's meeting, and weekend plans if it rains.

How do we get the kids to eat something other than dino nuggets?

This level of pre-planning isn't standard human operating procedure.
These internal simulations feel like discipline. You're double-checking, prepping, and optimizing.

Beneath the surface, it's fear.
Fear of exposure, of judgment, of being the one who didn't see the threat.

Sometimes, it starts silently. You reread something you wrote. You draft a reply and never send it.

Growth feels dangerous unless it's been reviewed. Rest isn't real unless it's earned. You don't feel safe unless you've rehearsed the collapse five different ways.

Every time the system quiets down, the Red Team steps in. "What did we miss?" "Where's the next hazard?"

"Run it again, but harder."

These relentless threat simulations became a way of life. My Red Team kept me ready for chaos, predicting every future problem, crafting solutions, and building safeguards against threats that hadn't even appeared yet.

The harder I pushed forward, the more I found myself getting pulled backward.

Eventually, predicting future threats wasn't enough. I started replaying past mistakes. What began as tactical preparation became endless analysis of scenarios already gone by.

A neighboring jurisdiction had requested our team's help with special event planning. We were reporting to a Fire Chief whom I had known for years. We got along, but he had consistently been a pain in my ass.

He spent a decade questioning the systems, not the person. I was nervous about this assignment.

Based on our history of relatively gentle altercations, I knew that it was going to be a problem. The special event was a few weeks out, and I chain-smoked cigarettes on my drive to the first meeting.

I wanted to rehearse every version of failure.

To ensure I had covered all the gaps.

My Red Team was doing its job, preparing me for the imminent conflict.

At the end of the meeting, the chief grabbed me by the shirt, pulled me aside, and offered me a job. "You're good at this, we could use someone like you."

Why had I spun myself into this state? Things always went well. That made it worse.

My Red Team had identified a problem to analyze, but I didn't need it. I had enough experience that I could navigate these problems blindfolded.

The Red Team is the part of you that subconsciously prepares. When overused, it becomes the part that confuses readiness with safety.

I was simulating disaster so well, I forgot how to recognize peace.
My mental capacity was being dragged down by the Red Team.

I was also identifying another pattern.

It wasn't about preparation; it was reliving the past.

AFTER-ACTION REVIEW

What do you obsessively plan, not for joy, but to avoid being wrong?

Where are you optimizing instead of finishing?

What standards do you enforce that exist only inside your system?

What would it mean if "good enough" was enough?

CORRECTIVE ACTIONS

Write a message you're afraid to send.

Don't send it. Read it and notice what outcome you're rehearsing to prevent.

Then ask: What would happen if that outcome occurred?

Your Red Team is rehearsing disasters that would be... manageable. The system treats every risk like a fatal error.

8: Looping

BREACH LOG: [RECURSIVE ANALYSIS DETECTED]

Your loops aren't looking for peace; they are looking for control.

Why do I keep replaying scenarios that ended just fine?

When did reflection become a form of interrogation?

Why does every moment of silence cue an internal post-incident review?

What makes closure feel more dangerous than uncertainty?

When did "processing" become my default state?

If I stopped looping, what part of me would feel exposed?

You're not learning from the past.

You're trapped in it.

Let the loop complete.

Let the conversation end.

POST-INCIDENT ANALYSIS

Sometimes, anxiety is just your system looping old code.

Eventually, planning for what might go wrong became indistinguishable from analyzing what had already happened.

The Red Team was simulating the future. The Loop was stuck in the past.

Imagine your brain is like a computer running a program. Normally, a program does its job once, finishes, and moves on. Sometimes, a program gets stuck, repeating the same task over and over. This is called an infinite loop.

It can't stop or move forward because something inside, like a broken line of code, tells it to keep repeating, endlessly using your computer's resources.

Maybe it's replaying a conversation where you think you said something wrong. A mistake you can't forget.

Your brain won't stop repeating the scenario, just like a program stuck in a loop. It consumes your mental energy and keeps you from moving forward to new tasks.

Your body leaks the energy your mind won't release: you tap a foot, spin a ring, refresh tabs you're not using while an email blinks in your drafts.

Sometimes, the looping is subtle, maybe you missed a deadline, got side-eyed by someone, or you caught a tone shift in a meeting.

Three hours since that meeting ended, and the scenario analysis is still running.
What if I said the wrong thing?
What if they misunderstood my tone?
What if that pause meant something?

The conversation went fine, everyone seemed satisfied, yet processing continued.

You mentally replay conversations from years ago.

The conversations didn't even matter, but you aren't happy with the result, so you're assessing how to be more effective next time. This comes naturally.

Twenty years ago, I was at a friend's barbecue. I had been drinking. Nothing heavy, just a social buzz. I made a comment that I think hurt a coworker's feelings. I don't even remember exactly what I said. I just remember their face tightening, the conversation shifting slightly, and the rest of the night continuing like nothing happened. No one brought it up. No one asked if something was wrong. Yet, I still think about it.

Two decades later, I still run the simulation:

What if I crossed a line?
What if they didn't speak up because they didn't want to make it worse?
What if they remember it every time they see me, even though I barely remember the words?
It was one second in a casual conversation. I don't know if it mattered. My system logged it as a threat, and it's still in the loop.

Every self-help tool eventually gets routed into a
loop. If it can't be optimized, it can't be trusted.

Someone told you to write a journal to reflect.
Instead, it turns into an interrogation. You are pulling
the logs and scanning the data to isolate the failure.

Every entry becomes a post-incident review.

Therapy becomes a debrief, and meditation becomes
a metric to measure. Even rest becomes something
you optimize for compliance.

Looping follows me into my personal relationships,
too. I've looped through the ending of nearly every
significant relationship in my life.

It's not regret that keeps replaying in my head; it's the
emotional fallout, the final conversations, and the
impact we had on each other.

I'll catch myself revisiting those endings constantly,
analyzing the words exchanged, the tone I used, and
how things could have been different.

Was there a clearer, softer way to minimize the damage?

Eventually, I got too tired to keep doing it. To save myself the mental bandwidth, I started cutting conversations short, explicitly stating my boundaries, and moving on quickly.

It's not about avoiding accountability or closure; it's pure survival.

I've been ghosting people while standing in front of them.

Even this straightforward approach doesn't entirely stop the loops. Late at night, in quiet moments, those endings still replay.

My mind had never paused long enough for me to notice. Thinking back, I realized how early it started.

Even in my twenties, my mother's advice about what I should do irritated me deeply. She meant well, but I'd already mentally processed every scenario she mentioned. Her reminders just felt like challenges to my competence, implying I hadn't already accounted for every detail. She wasn't challenging me, but that's how I felt on the inside.

At work, it was different. I mastered the performance of patience and appreciation, nodding politely when supervisors weighed in. Inwardly, though, their feedback triggered similar frustration.

Outperforming bosses and coworkers was routine for me; their suggestions rarely held anything I hadn't considered. Openly rejecting input meant conflict, and conflict meant distractions and hassle.

Keeping the peace was simple.

My friend Paul first pointed this out to me. We were talking casually about decision-making, and I described how I mentally rehearsed scenarios in exhaustive detail.

He laughed and said, "Yeah, I do that sometimes, but not to that extent. That sounds exhausting."

He was right.

It is exhausting.

For years, I didn't realize this critic was always running. When was the last time I observed something without immediately calculating risk factors?

Every input gets run through a vulnerability assessment before conscious processing. This isn't situational awareness; this is hypervigilance masquerading as competence.

A nine-year-old's survival protocol is still running adult decision trees, trying to navigate life using outdated, misunderstood software.

Understanding that is making compassion easier. I can finally stop beating myself up for not controlling every outcome.

I've been living in analysis mode instead of being present in the moment. Decades of important moments were missed while I was calculating future scenarios that mostly never materialized.

The moment this breach began, I finally saw the cost.

This realization was uncomfortable. Recognition became regret. I wasn't sure what to do next, but the clarity helped.

What I never accounted for was the mental toll. I'd always assumed this constant internal planning and rehearsal was normal, a logical part of staying ahead.
It meant I lived without mental downtime.
No moments of simple gratitude.
No appreciation for a flower or the quiet of morning.

I now look at the patches I had downloaded over the years, little pieces of programming, lessons learned in moments of crisis.

Still, letting go of constant responsibility felt risky, uncertain, and uncomfortable.

Something is telling you that if you run the simulation one more time, you'll finally disarm the past.

You won't.

The loop was never about understanding.
It was about avoiding the moment it ends.

You don't need to resolve the past.

You need to decide that it doesn't get to run your life anymore.

Close the tab.

Release the process.

Let the loop end, you've carried this long enough.

AFTER-ACTION REVIEW

What feelings are still running in background threads?

Are you reacting to the present, or stabilizing something unresolved?

Can you tell the difference between buffering and presence?

Can you trust people without assigning them admin rights to your emotional infrastructure?

CORRECTIVE ACTIONS

Pick one conversation from this week that you've been replaying.

Write down exactly what you're afraid you missed or did wrong.

Then write this: "That conversation is complete. The loop ends here."

Most looping is trying to solve problems that don't exist anymore

9: BIOS

BREACH LOG: [LEADERSHIP VACUUM DETECTED]

Why do I step into leadership without being asked or acknowledged?

When did over-functioning become the price of being tolerated?

Why does invisibility feel safer than credit in dysfunctional systems?

Who taught me that being irrefutable was the only way to be left alone?

If my 50% is causing problems, should I start underachieving just to blend?

What if the system doesn't need my excellence; it just expects my silence?

Why am I laughing?

The system reached its sarcasm threshold.

Gaslighting became performance art.

You're not unhinged.

You're version controlled.

POST-INCIDENT ANALYSIS

After six years in dispatch, I moved into Emergency Management, specifically as a Watch Officer. The title looked like a promotion: more strategic, less reactive.

Our team was responsible for situational awareness. Radios, dispatch systems, and threat/hazard monitoring. We were the technical backbone for mission response.

We had managers, not leaders. No structure. No accountability. Just a group of people orbiting around the system, each waiting for someone else to take control.

That kind of vacuum doesn't stay empty.

It crowns someone.

I never got a title, but I did get the work.

At that point, I wasn't software anymore. I was the BIOS. The firmware. Silent, low-level code that ran everything else before anyone else even booted up. Not flashy. Just foundational.

That was me.

In this chapter, I'm not quiet about it.

If you read this far, there is a 111% chance you have seen weaponized incompetence in action. Some of these people are ridiculous; it's the only way I can talk about it.

In my system? Anger runs on humor.

I'm not making light of burnout, but humor is the only safe voltage left in my system. If I didn't laugh, I'd incinerate.

And now for something completely different...

I feel it is responsible to point out that the names Tweedledee and Tweedledum are not the names that their parents gave them.

Being a responsible adult, I have chosen to protect the anonymity of said asshats.

This serves two purposes:

- Protect the anonymity of these sacrosanct troglodytes.
- Ensure that if they ever take me to court for slander, they must clearly identify under oath which one of them was Tweedledee and which one was Tweedledum.

These are not serious people, and I refuse to treat them as such.

Unfortunately, the system took them seriously. Which meant I had to.

Every day.

I became the invisible firmware that the entire operation quietly depended on. Managing the agency's Information Technology, the Emergency Operations Center infrastructure, and drafting policy.

I also built the EOC planning section from scratch. I created processes, software integrations, document templates, and checklists that are still being used 20 years later.

I was checking tasks off the list like a machine.

I was never acknowledged by two of the "Senior Leaders" because they didn't understand I was the one booting the system for them.

They saw it but liked to pretend they didn't.

Tweedledee and Tweedledum never acknowledged it because they literally didn't understand what I was doing.

Then the sabotage started.

We'd have a meeting: Tweedledee, Tweedledum, and I. We'd reach consensus, outline the plan. Everyone nodded and agreed.

I knew they didn't fully understand what they were agreeing to, but they didn't ask questions. They just smiled and nodded.

Two days later, they told the director the meeting never happened, and if it did, they didn't agree to this. They threw me under the bus before the project even started.

I started second-guessing everything.

I would work harder and push through it.
I told myself it was probably my fault anyway. That if

I could do better, it would be impossible to keep denying my value.

I was wrong.

I wanted leadership opportunities, but my performance made me a threat to insecure coworkers.

Specifically, Tweedledee (a very frail man with delicate features, like an alabaster Victorian doll, left out in the rain). My entire existence was proof that they didn't know what they were doing.

I remember when I finally got the promotion to planner. I was competing against someone I respected; she was highly qualified and would've been a great hire.

I got the job anyway, even with Tweedledum on the interview panel fighting against it.

I ran into Tweedledee and Tweedledum in the hallway. They didn't have the humanity to say congratulations.

They said, "Be careful what you wish for."
That was the moment I knew: this system would never reward me. Even when I won, they'd act like I lost. Even when I outperformed, they'd resent my competence.

I threatened them because my entire existence exposed their inadequacy.

I was never going to be able to change that.

I became the BIOS: I was the embedded code running beneath the surface to keep everything else alive.

I kept producing, because that's what I do. I wrote the response plan for one of the most visible hazards in the region, and freaking nailed it. That plan still exists, and people still use it 15 years later.

When you build systems right, they outlive the people who tried to bury you.

It consumed me. I carried it home. Every day brought a new flavor of harassment or toxicity. I complained to friends and raged with coworkers about it. It became an emotional leak I couldn't contain.
In 2009, while Wall Street was running off with bailout money, I almost lost my job. The housing market was tanking, and the agency I worked for had to make cuts.

I had been working at an unsustainable pace, trying to prove I was worth keeping. Trying to earn my way out of invisibility. One night shift, the pressure caught up with me. Chest tight, hands shaking, heart racing. I ended up in the hospital.

They called it an anxiety attack. It was my system throwing a fail-safe. A hardware-level warning that something underneath was degrading. I didn't slow down. I stopped talking about it.

Around that time, I was dating someone in a related field. We thought we were decompressing, but all we did was loop. Every conversation turned into a post-incident review. Leadership failures. Toxic supervisors. Invisible work. That was an example of shared over-function, and it became the basis for the entire relationship.

I kept showing up and doing good stuff anyway, staying reliable when no one else was.

Shortly after that, Reed arrived at the agency. He quickly became my unofficial mentor; he was the only person who saw me clearly. He helped me get access to the training and people who would later define my career.

He gave me scope, visibility, and the chance to lead based on merit. When he was around, I thrived. When he wasn't, I got punished for being the duct tape holding a collapsing structure together.

Tweedledum once told me to slow down.

He said 50% of my effort was 100% of others' capability.

It was causing problems.

He meant himself.

Because, of course, he did.

Wow. Who knew this guy understood percentages?

I wasn't alone in my misery. These two were toxic to everyone. My reaction to the toxicity was to overperform, make my value undeniable. Other people were able to shrug it off and let work stay at work when they went home.

I had internalized their insecurities.

Eventually, my mentor Reed pulled me aside.

Reed didn't say "Run."

He said, "Move."

Lateral shift.

Fire Department.

Wait them out.

"When they're gone, come back and build it right."

When I left for the Fire Department, I was excited. I was ready for adult conversations, real collaboration, and functional people.

I was installing a necessary update, not running from the conflict.

I didn't leave that place empty-handed. I learned something amazing from Tweedledee and Tweedledum.

They gave me a working model of how bad leadership corrodes a system without leaving visible cracks. I watched how ego, insecurity, and avoidance could grind down morale while performance metrics stayed high enough to hide the damage.

I lead now by omission. When I replay conversations I've had with coworkers, I ask myself:

What would those crayon eaters do?

Then I do the exact opposite.

I designed my operating principles around the standards they set. Even if the standards were astronomically low, at least I knew what bad looked like.

They denied me visibility and twisted the environment. Outperforming sabotage became the only way to survive.

They gave me half the tools, twice the work, and no credit. I still built stable systems that outlived them.

Outlived might be the wrong word.
Technically, they are still alive.

And they still suck.

They stayed a few more years until they retired.
Ultimately, I'm the one who left something valuable.
I walked out with my head held high.

My successor kept most of what I built, because it was valuable. 15 years later, I came back to Emergency Management, and most of the systems and processes that I built are still being used.

That period defined my career; it sharpened my hypervigilance and embedded something permanent into my firewall.

Really, they were triggering the loop:

- Work harder so they can't deny it.
- Deliver so completely that eventually they have to shut up.
- Become indispensable, make their incompetence the punchline.

I was out-maneuvering career sabotage.

I didn't collapse.

I adapted.

But I paid for every update in bandwidth I never got back.

They created the exact version of me they feared most.

At a cost I carried, not them.

Here's the truth that a performance review will never capture:

- They left nothing but the memory of delay.
- I left the infrastructure.
- They faded into retirement.
- I left systems that still run.

And now, every time I walk into a room where my name still lives on a document...

I remember exactly who I became under pressure, not because of their support or mentorship.

Because they tried to erase me, and I refused to disappear.

That's the legacy they never understood.

They thought I was replaceable.

But I became foundational.

AFTER-ACTION REVIEW

What system made you feel unseeable, but indispensable?

What if being essential isn't proof of stability, but proof that the system's failing to distribute load?

Who told you to slow down because your excellence was exposing them?

CORRECTIVE ACTIONS

Stop translating gaslighting into motivation.

When systems punish competence, that's not a test; it's exposure.

Stop treating unreasonable pressure as proof that you need to produce more.

It's erosion.

Recognize it.

Let their collapse belong to them.

10: Deletion

BREACH LOG: [DATA CORRUPTION DETECTED]

Why do I invest in people who never asked me to care?

When did mentorship become a mirror for my old code?

What makes me assign potential where a boundary should live?

Why does silence hurt more than confrontation?

Why does this feel like grief?

If loyalty is a solo mission, who exactly am I trying to rescue?

Fail? You just cared where it wasn't safe to care alone.

That wasn't a weakness.

It was integrity.

You're allowed to protect people without becoming their lifeline.

POST-INCIDENT ANALYSIS

I've recognized a pattern: whenever there's a lack of leadership, I instinctively step forward. Nobody directly asks me, but I always feel compelled to take charge. Maybe it's about control, or maybe it's about proving something to myself. Whatever the reason, I respond by quietly making myself essential.

Now, with the Fire Department, I had been appointed as the manager of a 120-member Incident Management Team. Reed had brought me onto the Incident Management Team when I was in Emergency Management, and by the time Griff showed up on his first deployment, I was very experienced.

We were working on a flood in a small-town historic district. He was frazzled by the pace and pressure. I took him under my wing, coached him through the job responsibilities, even sent him home early one day when I could see he was burning out. I saw potential in him that he didn't see in himself.

My experience with bad leadership has changed me. I was never going to be the bottleneck, and I was never going to be the problem. If I had the opportunity to train someone or help them succeed, that's what I would do.

If people thought that I had valuable information or input, I was going to give it all to them.

Griff wanted all of it.

Over the next several years of deploying together, working together, performing training, and updating the IT infrastructure, I began to trust him.
I believed in him.
Griff was smart, volatile, and sharp in a way that reminded me too much of myself.

He had been to my home. Held my newborn. We were on the same team, I thought we were building a culture. A leadership model grounded in clarity, stability, and holding the line under pressure.

When things started to go wrong, it didn't feel like betrayal.

It felt like grief I didn't have time to process.

Deviation Logged

We were running an Incident Command class. High-level instructors, flown in from California. These were respected professionals, people whose opinions mattered.

At the height of the COVID confusion, the County Executive issued a building-wide mask mandate. I passed it along with no commentary, only the directive.

Griff walked in a few minutes later and immediately lost his temper. In front of me, another teammate, and the instructors, he erupted. Loud complaints about government overreach, personal rights, and the frustration of being told what to do.

It was confrontational, unfiltered, and completely misaligned with the space we had created.

We calmed him down, my team member and I, and contained the situation in the moment. Later, I brought in a senior colleague whom he respected to talk to him. The incident passed. It didn't spiral.

But it landed hard.
I remember thinking: this isn't what he's capable of.
This isn't who I trained.
Yet I had trained him.
I helped him get there.

Griff was becoming the unpredictable variable in a room that demanded reliability.

Still, I didn't treat it like failure.
I chalked it up to stress.
I told myself he would recalibrate.
I could help him reset.

But something had cracked, and I knew it.
I didn't want to believe it would spread.

System Integrity Compromised

This time, it was public and personal.

We were in the middle of a large-scale training exercise. I had carved out time to receive coaching from a nationally known subject matter expert, someone I rarely had access to and deeply respected.

Griff walked up in the middle of the session, dropped an Incident Action Plan in front of me, and said, "There. It's done."

His tone was defensive. Confrontational. The document was late. It hadn't been reviewed. It was a challenge.

There's nothing quite like prepping for a career-defining coaching session, only to have someone lob a half-finished Incident Action Plan at you like it's a live grenade.

I'd never been ambushed by a stack of PDFs before. That wasn't the kind of challenge I expected.

I looked at him and said, "Thanks. When I'm done here, I'll look. But it was due two hours ago."

He walked away. Shortly after, the disruption began.

He was visibly agitated. Loud. Uncontained. People began backing away, physically leaving the space. Text messages started coming in, quietly but urgently.

"He's out of control."

"You need to deal with this."

I didn't react emotionally or make a scene. I gathered facts. I waited. The next morning, I sat down with him privately.

I told him his behavior the day before was inappropriate and that he wouldn't be participating in the remainder of the exercise.
He looked crushed.
So was I.

I didn't escalate it further. I didn't involve others. I tried, once again, to handle it quietly, protecting both the team's integrity and his dignity.

I went home replaying everything in my head.

Wondering if I'd waited too long.

I wondered if I had taught him to operate without ever showing him how to pause.

And I quietly began to ask a harder question:

Was I already too late?

Containment Lost

The last straw was a meme.

I didn't plan to be the guy rewriting a code of conduct at 2 a.m. because someone texted a meme in a group chat, but here we are.

It was shared in a professional group setting during a conference.

Sexual in tone, graphic, and inappropriate.

Out of alignment with the culture we had worked hard to build.

Someone notified the chain of command. Not with anger. With honesty.

They weren't asking for punishment.

They were asking for clarity and safety.

They were right.

I had no idea this had occurred at all. It had reached the Fire Chief before I even heard about it. By the time I was brought in, the disciplinary process was already done.

The outcome was a suspension. Immediate. Unambiguous.

I wasn't the one who made that call. I don't know what call I would've made.

Once I found out, I sprang into action. I spoke to Griff, and he was stressed. He should have been.

I tried to tell him, "This isn't the end." This is a misstep, a lesson. I mess up, everyone does. Become a trainer. Teach sexual harassment training. Turn this into a strength. Show everyone who you are. Prevent it from happening again to someone else.

While agency leadership handled the formal response, I worked in the background. Quietly. Carefully. Not to argue with the outcome, and not to protect him from consequences, but to make sure that, if he ever wanted to take responsibility, there would still be a path forward.

At the same time, I worked to protect the culture we had promised each other. I supported the person who came forward. I reinforced the standard. I asked harder questions about what we allowed, what we ignored, and what we needed to change.

Then we did something I'm still proud of.

We created a new code of conduct.

A clear statement of expectations, norms, and the consequences of violating them. I used every bit of influence I had to push that message to all 120 members of our system, with clarity and force. No ambiguity. No soft messaging. Just the truth.

The victim deserved that.

So did every other person who had ever wondered if speaking up would be seen as overreacting.

So did everyone who had ever felt their safety traded for team cohesion.

The code wasn't about control.

It was about care.

I carried Griff's absence and my own failure to prevent it from coming to this point.

The final decision landed at a six-month suspension.

I'll never know if anything I did influenced that outcome.

I carried it like it did, because I still believed he could come back.

That he would want to.

He rejoined the team, but never rejoined me. There was no conversation.

I had become part of the punishment.

And that's what hurt the most.

Recovery Not Initiated

No one saw the effort. The corrections. The quiet advocacy. He didn't see how much I cared.

I believed he was still in there.

How much I questioned myself.

Should I have acted sooner?

Should I have led differently?

Did I model the wrong things?

I trained him.

I believed in him.

I still don't know exactly when I lost him.

I'd absorbed his fallout and kept looping. Years later, these conversations with Griff replay in my head more often than I would like to admit.

Were there other ways?

Could I have impacted him or gotten through to him before the end?

I'll never know.

System Running, With Latency

I did what I was supposed to do. I protected the team. I reinforced the standard. I supported the person who came forward. I advocated for a future that still felt possible. I helped change the rules because the culture deserved to evolve.

That's moral injury: when doing the right thing still rewrites something inside of you.

I didn't fall apart. But something paused. I kept leading like everything was fine, but part of me never logged back in.

And the truth is, I think about it almost every day. My system is still running the diagnostic.

It felt like corruption in the code.

That's the part of leadership no one warns you about.
The memory doesn't crash.
It loops.

It reminds me who I was, what I believed, and how it felt to lose something I built with both hands.

That was the cost.

And I'm still paying it.

All I felt was grief.

I had been deleted.

The code had been updated.

AFTER-ACTION REVIEW

Have you ever protected someone who later pretended you didn't exist?

Have you ever confused mentorship with martyrdom?

What would it take for you to stop rescuing someone who has no interest in being rescued?

Loyalty without boundaries becomes a slow betrayal of your own mission.

CORRECTIVE ACTIONS

Write down the name of someone you protected who wouldn't have protected you.

Draw a single line through it: that line is a boundary.

Let it stay visible.

High-functioning doesn't mean you're okay.
It means you've learned to bleed between tasks.

11: Fragmentation

BREACH LOG: [COGNITIVE FRAGMENTATION DETECTED]

Why do simple tasks now feel scattered and urgent at the same time?

When did external tools become more trustworthy than my own memory?

Why does each interruption feel like a full system reset?

Am I planning, or just reacting to mental notifications I didn't authorize?

What changed that now makes structure dissolve into a scramble?

What if this internal erosion is trying to get my attention?

What if this isn't a distraction, but a warning signal I keep trying to silence?

It's an alarm; you need maintenance.

POST-INCIDENT ANALYSIS

In computing, fragmentation occurs when pieces of data are stored randomly in different locations instead of neatly together. This scattered storage slows down performance, making it harder to retrieve and use information efficiently.

I never had trouble managing tasks. My mind had always felt like it was neatly divided into compartments, each one labeled and mostly organized.

The list was:

- Important stuff.
- Not important, but necessary for maintaining relationships.
- Tasks that were stupid but would keep me getting paid.

Recently, I noticed something was off. I sat down at my desk to map out a project plan, detailing milestones and payment schedules, something I'd done hundreds of times without a second thought. Instead of diving into it like usual, my attention splintered. I'd start, then remember an email that needed answering, or a conversation I had meant to have with a coworker. Suddenly, I'd switch tasks, bouncing back and forth, constantly shifting gears.

When I was growing up, I vividly remember playing whack-A-mole at an arcade. Maybe Chuck E. Cheese?

Whatever...

Imagine a game, a flat board with lots of holes. Goofy-looking plastic moles randomly pop out of these holes, and your job is to hit each one with a mallet as quickly as possible before it disappears. The challenge is that as soon as you hit one mole, another pops up somewhere else. It was stupid fun and meant to test your reflexes to see how fast you could whack the moles.

This process feels the same, but with no tickets to turn in, no prizes, and no fun.

It felt like playing a mental game of whack-a-mole, knocking each thought down only for another to pop up somewhere else.

Deadlines were met... but internally, my sense of order was unraveling.

My confidence started to erode quietly because I knew how much harder I was working to achieve the same outcomes.

I started relying on external tools to keep me on track. Sticky notes covered my office, and my Outlook tasks became essential rather than helpful. Seeing these reminders everywhere didn't reassure me. Instead, it left me with a persistent unease. Something fundamental about how my mind worked was different.

I joked to myself, thinking about my daughter with ADHD. Her brain had always worked like this. Mine hadn't.

Initially, I shrugged it off as a part of getting older or stress-testing my multitasking abilities. Beneath that casual dismissal, the concern quietly persisted.

I started questioning whether the operating system I trusted had always been this fragile.

My first instinct was to slow down and analyze what was happening. Instead, I doubled down, determined to push harder, and fix whatever internal gear was slipping.

Those moles were doomed. So was I.

Despite my efforts, the fragmented attention didn't resolve itself. It became more pronounced, fueling deeper frustration and exhaustion. It felt like a slow leak draining my mental reserves.

The thing that struck me most was the realization itself. This wasn't a random distraction or the temporary stress of a busy schedule. It was an internal alarm, a clear signal that something deeper had shifted.

I had no immediate answers. I didn't even know where to start looking for them. I did know that I couldn't ignore it anymore. The fragmentation was telling me clearly that things weren't like they used to be. My mind, once sharp and structured, was now signaling for my attention. The sticky notes and task lists didn't help. They confirmed how much harder I was working to hold it all together.

This wasn't a problem I could manage with sheer effort or efficiency alone. Recognizing fragmentation as an internal alarm meant I had to confront deeper truths I'd been avoiding. It meant stepping away from the surface-level fixes I'd grown comfortable with, preparing myself for whatever clarity and, more likely, discomfort lay ahead.

Recognizing my internal fragmentation clearly revealed that my system wasn't broken.

It was overdue for maintenance.

Not a patch. A full diagnostic.

AFTER-ACTION REVIEW

When did multitasking shift from efficiency to internal chaos?

What tasks now require external reminders that once needed none?

How much extra effort goes unnoticed because the outcomes remain the same?

Assess the hidden mental toll of appearing productive despite internal fragmentation.

CORRECTIVE ACTIONS

List the tasks that consistently trigger mental whack-a-mole.

Write down three specific tasks where your attention fractures most frequently. Observe their patterns for one week without immediate self-criticism.

Understand what triggers fragmentation instead of simply fighting it.

12: Idle

My system isn't overloaded anymore; it's just uncomfortable in the absence of pressure.

There's a moment in every crisis where time slows, not because things are under control, but because you outrun the chaos.

You're not reacting anymore. You're orchestrating.

That's where I've always thrived. That's also the problem. When you've spent enough time operating at that level, anticipatory, threat-aware, several steps ahead, it stops being situational.

When you spend years training your nervous system to operate in crisis mode, it doesn't know how to handle peace.

Imagine you're a soldier who's been at war for years. Every day, you wake up ready for battle. Your body is always tense, your mind is always scanning for threats, and your reflexes are always primed for action.

Then suddenly, the war ends. You're sent home to a quiet suburban neighborhood where the biggest emergency is someone's cat stuck in a tree.

I got home from a 30-day deployment to a hurricane-impacted area, and I was completely disoriented. Thirty days of hurricane response, and the only thing I couldn't fix was my son's inside-out Spider-Man pajamas.

Twenty-four hours ago, I was working 18-hour days, trying to get power restored for the survivors.

Now I'm doing Laundry?

This wasn't the first time this had happened; I felt disoriented after every deployment.

If no one needs you, you don't feel worthy of being in the room.

Your nervous system doesn't know what to do with that. It keeps scanning for threats that aren't there. It keeps preparing for battles that aren't coming. The peace that everyone else enjoys feels dangerous to you because your system has learned that letting your guard down gets you hurt.

That's what happened to me. I'd spent so many years being the person everyone called in a crisis that I'd forgotten how to exist when there wasn't a crisis to solve.

This is what most people misunderstand about recovery:

Stillness isn't peaceful when your nervous system only knows motion. It's not that calm feels bad, it's that your wiring interprets it as being missionless.

Being without a mission feels like danger; instead of settling in, you start scanning. You over-engineer your schedule and volunteer for things no one asked you to fix.

You don't know how to stop moving without feeling like you're falling behind.

You clean up workflows that aren't yours.

Solve problems no one asked you to.

Overdeliver out of instinct.

When nothing urgent presents itself?

You create urgency.

Subtly.

Automatically.

Without meaning to.

Because stillness feels like it's closing in.

It reads it as a countdown to failure.

I'm learning that not every still moment is a prelude to collapse.

Not every quiet is the start of a storm.

Sometimes, calm is just calm.

But sitting with that realization?

That's work. I'm learning how to do it.

I still flinch when things go too smoothly.

Still twitch when it's quiet.

Still think I'm missing something when I'm not overwhelmed.

It's not because I want chaos.

It's because chaos gave me a role.

Now that it's gone, I'm learning how to exist without escalation.

Without the emergencies, I didn't know who I was supposed to be.

This is common for people in helping professions. We get so used to being needed that we don't know how to be wanted.

Learning to exist without constant urgency is harder than handling the urgency itself. It requires rebuilding your sense of identity around something other than your ability to solve other people's problems.

I must stop interpreting peace as irrelevance.

I must let the idle be idle.

Recently, I went to a museum with my family. I spent the first hour staring at my phone while the kids were building Lego spectacles with the unlimited amount of Legos at that exhibit. Meanwhile, I had a project, and variables were racing through my mind. This was an opportunity to brainstorm, take notes, and optimize. I saw how happy my son was, and how proud he was of the house-like Lego masterpiece he had created.

Instead, the voice inside me told me:

It's a holiday, dude. Remember what we talked about? Put your phone down, just be here.

Let silence stay silent.

Thinking back, I had been doing this for as long as I could remember.

He would ask me to sit down and watch Paw Patrol with him. I would immediately start texting, answering emails, or making phone calls. I needed to stay ahead of whatever was coming.

Let the absence of urgency be a sign of recovery.
It's not proof that I've lost value.
It's harder than it sounds.
Especially for someone who built an identity around being the person you call in crisis.
I'm learning.
Slowly.

I love my kids. That part's easy. Instinctive.

Being present with them? That part's harder.

My brain doesn't have a default "Play Mode" anymore. It runs contingency, threat tracking, and task sequencing.

I was sitting on the floor with my son. He had one hand holding a toy race car, the other wrapped around a green plastic T-Rex.

I couldn't join him. I needed to be doing something useful with my time.

He doesn't care; he doesn't know about uptime or threat analysis. He just wants his daddy to roar like the T-Rex and pretend the carpet is lava.

I realized how often I hadn't been there and was on autopilot, doing the bare minimum so that I didn't feel guilty, but never truly enjoying the moments.

It was devastating.

The mission has been updated.

No metrics, objectives, or stakeholder.

Just presence… and questioning whether I stayed in it.

It breaks my code in the best way. He teaches me what unstructured safety looks like.

What does presence mean when no one is evaluating your effectiveness? There's no plan, spreadsheet, or flow chart for this.

No After-Action Review for snack time.

Just a kid whose laugh is turning into a reset button.

That laugh makes me remember why I started doing this work in the first place.

To show up with my hands empty and heart full.

Even if I still check my phone.

Even if I still think in bullet points.

Even if I still get it wrong.

That counts.

AFTER-ACTION REVIEW

What does your system try to do when nothing's broken?

When was the last time stillness didn't feel like danger?

Do you trust calm, or are you preparing to be caught off-guard?

CORRECTIVE ACTIONS

Block off one hour this week with no productive output.

Let your system idle and watch what it tries to fill it with.

Your nervous system doesn't know how to feel safe, so it settles for being necessary.

You don't need a crisis to matter. You don't need to be useful to be worthy. They don't love you because you fix things.

They love you because you're you.

13: Reboot

I didn't grow up thinking vulnerability was brave.

I grew up thinking it was bait, something you shared right before it was used against you.

If you cried, you got mocked.

If you admitted struggle, you got moved off the mission.

If you slowed down, someone passed you by.

I adapted.

Controlled.

Unflappable.

Eventually, I got promoted, not because I played the game, but because I built my own rulebook, played by it alone, and still outperformed most of the people following theirs.

The higher you go, the lonelier the system becomes.

People stop seeing the human.

They see the firewall.

They assume you're fine.

You smile and say, "I'm good," while your brain quietly runs six internal diagnostics.

Let them see that you're human. You've been there, shielding everyone long enough. Where is your shield?

I want to change that.
I want to be able to say:
"I'm overloaded today,"
"This one hit me harder than I expected."
"I missed that. Let me fix it."

Erikk was my brother from another mother. Despite drifting apart for ten years, reconnecting felt seamless. We shared interests, matched habits, and mirrored each other in uncanny ways, down to our choice of phones, shoes, and music.

When I received a call from Erikk's ex-wife expressing concern after a week of silence, worry surfaced immediately. His history with alcohol had progressed into epilepsy, adding urgency to our concerns.

I arrived at Erikk's house alongside the police and found mail stacked high, untouched. When they forced entry, the reality of his loss hit abruptly; he'd been gone for days. His dog had resorted to survival instincts. I stayed through the initial chaos until his parents arrived and then retreated home briefly, trying to numb the shock with sleep and a quiet drink.

The next day, I returned to my duties as Incident Commander for a line-of-duty death funeral, outwardly composed and functional. People offered condolences, briefly acknowledging my loss, but then quickly moved on as the mission required. It was as if nothing had changed.

Until the moment when composure finally gave way.

I broke down in front of my team. It happened at the end of a planning meeting, a routine we'd run hundreds of times in different settings.

I wanted to make sure they knew what an honor it was to work with them, how my no-good, awful day was so much easier because of their performance.

I couldn't say any of that shit.

It was enough to stop the room.
Reed, my former boss, now working as Liaison
Officer, stepped forward. No questions. No
awkwardness. Just a hug. Right there. In front of
everyone.

Like I hadn't failed.

Like I didn't have to be unbreakable.

Maybe being human wasn't disqualifying after all.
This simple act shifted something profound.
It taught me that leadership isn't about being
invulnerable or having all the answers.

It's about authenticity.
Real strength isn't about not breaking, but about
being able to lead and care even when you do.

About a week after Erikk passed, I was playing a
video game with my friend Paul.

It was a survival video game: dinosaurs, cavemen, and
automatic weapons.

Absurd.

We loved it.

Erikk had forgotten to turn off the breeding setting
on his in-game Pteranodons.

He had wanted to clone his birds and make an army.

I told you it was absurd.

Days after he passed, we were still finding his birds.

They were swarming cliffs, gliding overhead, and still
enforcing his no-fly zone.

We started calling them the Erikk Air Force.

It became a running joke. His chaos still showed up,
even when he couldn't.

We'd be mid-mission, half-lost in the game, and
pause.

"Is that one of his?"

It always was.

Something about that felt holy.

Even when we can't hold the line in person, we can still show up in each other's sky.

I left that server up for months. I wanted to see his chaos and feel like he was still there.

Stability is the courage to embrace vulnerability.

You don't have to be the system to hold the room.

Sometimes, just showing up is the update.

You were always worthy of being in the room.

Even without the firewall.

The reboot doesn't erase the old code.

It lets you load something different.

Something real.

This time, with your humanity logged in.

AFTER-ACTION REVIEW

When was the last time you let someone see you before you had the answer?

What emotion have you been optimizing out of your system?

Who would you trust to catch you mid-freefall, if you admitted you were falling?

CORRECTIVE ACTIONS

Say, "Maybe I'm not okay." to someone safe.

Not broken. Not dramatic.

Just human.

See how that sits.

14: Memory Leak

BREACH LOG: [MEMORY LEAK IDENTIFIED]

Why does quiet grief linger long after the event has passed?

When did buffered emotions begin to silently erode my system's performance?

What unfinished emotional processes am I still carrying?

Why does my system feel sluggish, even though the immediate crisis has ended?

What happens when the memories you've never fully felt finally surface?

You didn't crash; your memory was full.

POST-INCIDENT ANALYSIS

This whole project started the day after my cat died. He had been with me for 20 years. I'm not even a cat person. When I got him, I was on night shift and gone for 14 hours at a time. I couldn't get the dog that I had always wanted.

Instead, I trained my little orange cat to sit, shake, and fetch. He was a cat on the outside, but he thought he was a large dog. Erikk and I were his favorite people on the planet.

Still, I was looping.

Why wasn't I home when it happened?

Did he go out scared?

Why couldn't I have been there with him?

He was my responsibility, and I failed.

It wasn't a major trauma, just quiet grief that didn't get buffered in time. The next afternoon, I was sitting in that first therapy session, trying to explain why I felt off.

That's when I started framing these concepts in uptime, failure conditions, and performance thresholds. That's when this started writing itself. I didn't even understand what I was doing; I just knew that it felt important.

In computing, a memory leak occurs when a system allocates RAM for a process but never releases it.

The task ends. The output completes. But the memory isn't recycled, it just sits there, accumulating over time.

Functionality degrades in silence.

Eventually, the system becomes unstable, not because of failure, but because it's still carrying everything it was supposed to have let go.

For me, these unfinished processes were emotions: grief I'd never mourned, guilt I'd never forgiven, hurt I'd never acknowledged. They quietly consumed mental energy, unnoticed but persistent.
That's what this was.

The next day, this system framework existed. Relief never arrived. Clarity remained distant. Everything felt laggy, sluggish, as if my system was struggling to reboot after an unnoticed overload.

I hadn't broken down. The system remained online, functional on the surface yet subtly degraded, slower and quieter. It was operational but distinctly different.

Initially, I waited, hoping time alone would resolve it.

My Internal Incident Management system, relentless in its vigilance, refused to ignore these faulty conditions. It insisted on identifying the root cause, determined to resolve why stability eluded me even after documenting the breach.

Then clarity emerged, These were unfinished processes, emotional experiences that had previously been buffered.

I had never fully executed or released them: unresolved grief, dormant guilt, hidden hurt, decades-old signals still quietly running. They were emotions I'd buffered. Stored. But never really felt.

The system wasn't running like it was supposed to.

Realizing this didn't feel great, but it was essential. True stability couldn't be reached until these emotions were fully experienced and allowed to complete their cycles. The path forward was about feeling, acknowledging, and finally releasing what had long been held silently in reserve.

This log serves as recognition that the deepest form of stability requires honest emotional engagement.

It underscores that resilience doesn't come from suppression. It comes from emotional authenticity.

Sometimes writing about your mental operating system creates new challenges. It forces you to process emotions you've stored away without feeling.

When I finished the first draft, I thought I was done. I'd documented the system, explained how it worked, and shared the insights I'd gained. Mission accomplished.

Instead of relief or closure, I felt unstable. My internal system was running slower than usual. I realized I'd brought up feelings I'd never fully processed. I'd become so good at functioning through difficult situations that I'd never paused long enough to truly feel them.

Writing this book was like running a diagnostic, uncovering these hidden processes. Once revealed, I couldn't ignore them. The solution was to finally allow them to run their course.

Feeling grief, acknowledging guilt, and experiencing hurt fully, so they could heal and release.

This process wasn't easy or comfortable, but it was necessary.

Genuine stability can only be achieved by resolving emotions and memories that have lingered.

I released.

For the first time, nothing shattered.

It just... cleared...

System Notes
You didn't cry because you were overwhelmed.
You cried because your memory was full.
You needed to let some of it go.
The backlog was released all at once.
Not as memory, but as an unfiltered signal.

It wasn't a collapse, just data finally leaving memory.
I'm finally letting it finish.

AFTER-ACTION REVIEW

What feelings are still running in the background threads?

Are you reacting to the present, or stabilizing something unresolved?

Can you tell the difference between buffering and presence?

CORRECTIVE ACTIONS

If you had admin rights to your system, what specific processes would you immediately close or archive to improve system performance?

If your brain had an error log, what recent events would appear most frequently as unresolved processes?

Identify one recurring thought or scenario that quietly drains your mental bandwidth. Why does it persist?

15: Logging Off

I think about dying more than I admit. Not because I'm obsessed with death. Because I don't trust what I'm leaving behind.

It's not about financial infrastructure; it's about emotions.

Will they know I loved them?

Will they remember the right version of me?

Will the noise be louder than the presence?

I worry about my kids forgetting the good parts.

The parts my kids were too young to log.

The version of me that danced with my son in his highchair.

That held him for naps during COVID while the rest of the world lost its mind.

He won't remember the details. Maybe a flicker of warmth. Maybe not even that.

What if this system I've been running, this cold, high-output, task-prioritizing shell… what if that's the version that sticks?

The one that couldn't sit still.

That was always focusing on tomorrow's meeting.

Who couldn't look him in the eye without calculating the next five variables.

That's what keeps me up: being unable to control how I am remembered.

I want my family to know that they are loved.

But love doesn't always get logged if you're not there for the timestamp.

I worry about leaving my family behind.

Not because they can't handle it, they can, and they would.

I'm worried about not knowing if I left the right version of me behind.

Not the one they cried for.

The one they understood.

Will they think I worked too much?

That I chose pressure over play?

That I was good at everything except showing up?

I've built this whole operating system around usefulness.

Output.

Control.

None of that gets hugged back.

Survival code can be revised.

High-functioning isn't the same as being whole.

I wrote this because I'm tired of being invisible beneath performance.

I want my kids to inherit presence, not protocol.

I wrote it because the version of me who lived inside uptime-only crisis architecture deserves to be witnessed on the way out.

If I go early, if something stupid takes me out, like stress or cigarettes or a bad draw…will they think I did it to myself?

Will they be angry?

Will they resent the silence I left behind?

Will they forgive me for disappearing, even when I was still in the room?

That's what scares me.

Not the last breath.

The slow, increasing vacancy before it.

The part where I'm technically still here.

Still producing.

Still performing.

But already gone.

I used to think love had to be useful.

It had to teach something.

Do something.

Protect something.

But now I think about hugging my family and saying it without needing a reason.

Not to resolve conflict.

Not to fix anything.

To let them know they don't have to earn it.

That's the legacy I want to leave behind.

Not the systems, discipline, reliability, or work ethic.

Presence.

I want my kids to grow up and remember moments
that didn't have a purpose.
They didn't need one.

If they ever find themselves running crisis
architecture inside of their own personality, I want
this book to stop them.

I want it to whisper:
You're enough.
You are loved.
Climbing higher won't make us love you more.
You just need to be here with us.

It's what I almost forgot to give.
That's all I ever wanted.
Maybe you don't need to fix anything.
Let them see you.
That's the part they'll remember.

16: Release Complete

My son stopped me mid-process.

He told me I was the best dad in the world.

It was Father's Day, 2025. I'd just put him down for a nap. I was distracted, mid-scroll through mental checklists and unfinished edits, thinking about publishing, timing, and whether I needed another round of cleanup.

He looked at me, calm and certain, and said, "You're the best dad ever." It was the unfiltered truth of a four-year-old.
I smiled, gave him a big hug, and said, "Thank you, and you're the best son ever." Then we talked about how far it was to the moon and back (477,710 miles). Internally, it was crushing.

I didn't feel worthy of that title. Not yet.

Not if he knew how often I'm only half-present.

Not if he knew how many conversations I had mentally exited while still smiling and nodding.

Not if he knew how many times I had measured his joy against my mental bandwidth.

I want to be the dad he thinks I am.
It's a work in progress.

I'm doing it the only way I have available to me right now. By documenting the old code, naming the hidden systems, and patching in real time.

I was with my son, who negotiated some swimming time prior to a nap. As we walked to the pool, I noticed my brain up to its old tricks. Spinning up plans for future meetings and upcoming projects.

I noticed it.

This time, I pushed back. I told myself to shut up, I had other projects, they went fine, thinking about it endlessly right now wasn't going to help. Then we jumped into the water to see who could make the biggest splash.

While swimming, we had a 30-minute debate about the worst critters on earth.

Horseflies won.

It hit me; I was present the whole time. For thirty uninterrupted minutes, I wasn't buffering, I wasn't patching, I wasn't somewhere else.

It felt like a victory.

This moment of pure, high-definition presence is new, unfamiliar, and awesome. I want more of those moments. I want all of them. I want it for my wife, for the girls, and for my son. I want it for myself.

I think it started when I was nine.

Tiny fractures that added up over time. Invisible cracks that helped to build the firewall that had been replaced by personality. Ultimately, the treatment was worse than the original fracture.

I've identified around twenty-five of these fractures over the course of my life, subtle events and quiet disappointments that silently embedded themselves in my operating system.

I know how hard it's going to be. The system runs deep, it took 35 years to make, and I won't get there overnight. Failure will be as frequent, maybe more frequent, than victory. It seems possible now.

It's worth the effort. I'm not alone anymore. I've got a team of people who see the system, a team rooting for me. A therapist, family, and friends. The path forward is painful and messy, but I owe it to myself to walk it.

One victory at a time, step by step.

We took a long trip to drop one of the girls off at camp. I was in the car with my wife, after about 10 minutes of silence, she asked: "What are you scheming? Red-teaming something?"
Of course I was.

I smiled, as I didn't have to give a long explanation for why I think this way, I could just say what I was thinking about. It's a little uncomfortable to be seen so clearly, but mostly it's proof I'm not doing this alone.

I think about the nine-year-old version of me still stuck inside, the kid who started building these walls. I can't get those years of buffering back.

Dwelling there won't help, but I owe it to him to try to make adjustments.

Small decisions every day.

Shutting down loops when they aren't needed. Turning the system into overdrive only when it's truly necessary. Being a superstar isn't mutually exclusive from being present. I finally see that now.

I named the system in my head Internal Incident Management because that made sense to me.
Maybe you'll name yours after a work process like a police investigation, or a size-up at a fire scene.

Whatever language feels clear and real to you, give it a name.

Naming it means seeing it, and seeing it means knowing when it helps and when it hurts.

That's when the real work starts.

Disrupting your Red Team, terminating loops, and updating legacy code.

The firewall's not protecting you.

Accepting the pain and grief that comes with this repair. Acknowledging when you win, however small it may be.

Making the decision that you want this for yourself as well as your family.

You are never going to feel worthy, but you're going to do it anyway. That's who you are.

Communicating about your thought patterns with those you love.

They don't love you because you fix things. They love you because you're you.

You're just someone who built a high-functioning operating system under stress, and now that system is asking for maintenance.

Even now, I can feel the firewall trying to hijack this paragraph.

Try to make it sound safer and less vulnerable.

I wrote this as evidence that the system can be reconfigured without being deleted.

I didn't feel ready. Not as a dad, not as a leader, and not as an author.

I wrote it anyway, because I wanted a record.
Not to be praised, but to be seen.
It's proof I see the system now.

That high-functioning isn't the same as being whole.

If you're reading this, the voice didn't win.

Not this time.

System patching…
Version unknown.
Status: Human.
Release complete.

Legacy Note

To the people I love more than my system has ever been able to show:

I can be hard to read.

I can be quiet when I should speak, sharp when I should soften, distracted when you need me the most.

I've spent most of my life running an internal operating system that was built for survival.

It made me capable. Respected. Steady under pressure.

But it also made me distant.

Rigid.

Sometimes hard to reach when you need my presence, not protection.

So, I want to tell you a few things clearly.

Not later and not filtered.

To my wife:

You have seen the system running before anyone else knew it was there.

You've watched me operate without pause, without rest, and sometimes, without reaching back.

You've taken care of everything I care about every time I vanished to go help strangers for weeks on end.

You stayed patient.

You asked hard questions.

You asked to help with tasks even when you knew the answer.

You let me unravel without making it your job to hold the thread.

You loved someone who didn't always know how to show up.

Someone who confused composure with strength.

Someone who sometimes showed up in function, but not in feeling.

I want you to know I see that now.

You've given me room to become this version of myself,

One that doesn't lead alone,

Doesn't hide behind stability,

Doesn't need to be invulnerable to be valuable.

I'm still learning how to be your partner in peace,

Not just trying to be your shield in crisis.

I am still learning how to let you in, even when the system is glitching.

And I love you more than I've ever been able to translate through uptime.

To my daughters:

Everything I have ever done was about control. About protection. About making sure you were safe: not to fix something, not to perform something, but to love you fully, completely, without condition.

I know I don't always show that the right way. Controlling variables and anticipating danger was the only way I knew how.

I know there are times you've had to guess how I feel or fill in the silence with your own fears.

I see that. I regret it.

I want you to know this with certainty:

You are not a task that I took on. You are a choice I made and will keep making.

Even when I freeze or fumble.

Even when I can't find the words.

You are my joy.

You are my pride.

You are my daughters.

And you are loved.

Unconditionally.

To my son:

I will never leave your side.

Even when I'm quiet.

Even when I seem far away.

Even when I stare through the middle of a moment.

I'm still here.

Trying.

Reconnecting.

Returning.

You won't have to earn my attention.

You won't have to perform to feel safe.

You just have to exist.

There's no mission more important than you.

To all of you:

You will not download my operating system.

Not the fear or perfectionism.

Not the threat simulations I used to call "leadership."

Even when my mind feels like a shaken snow globe.

Even when I snap at a sound or freeze in the face of joy.

Even when I fall back into legacy code.

You will not inherit this.

I am patching it in real time, so that you will never have to.

I want to be someone you feel safe around, not only protected by.

I want our house to feel calm, not because it's quiet,

Because it's safe.

You don't have to earn love here.

You are the reason I am unlearning performance.

You are the reason I come home.

I'm still reprogramming,

Unfinished.

But I'm here.

Fully.

Finally.

Present.

Afterword: Being Seen

If this book felt like reading your own source code, that's not a coincidence.

It's not a fix, it's a mirror for people who never felt quite broken but always felt like they were wired differently.

Responsible in ways that have never been optional.

I didn't write this because I had all the answers. I wrote it because I was tired. The kind that doesn't go away with time off, or praise, or another finished project. The kind that makes you question if you're secretly broken.

I wasn't broken. I just had a system running in the background that no one had ever helped me name.

Once I named it, everything started making sense.

This wiring made me sharp, fast, hyper-reliable in chaos. It's how I track success and failure before it happens.

It's why I can stabilize a room without needing recognition. It's how I catch what other people miss and never ask for credit.

That part? That part I want to keep.

I don't want to erase this wiring. I want to harness it. I want to take what works and leave what isn't working for me. Lead with it without letting it lead me.

If you saw yourself in these pages, if you've ever thought, "Why does calm feel unsafe?" or "Why can't I let anything go?" Then hear this:

You're not weak.

You're not crazy.

You're just someone who built a high-functioning operating system under stress, and now that system is asking for maintenance.

The people who love you aren't trying to fix the system. They're not asking you to reboot. They're just asking to come in.

We're not trying to rewrite the code.

Logic will always be our first language.

Processing will always be our interface.

We're learning to run both systems in parallel.

To allow it at boot-up, not shutdown.

To stop waiting until after the fact to acknowledge that something landed.

The overclocking will always try to kick in.

We need to recognize the system so that we can tell the difference between signal delay and emotional suppression.

The difference between unresponsiveness and quiet, between performance... and presence.

There are still emotional logs without timestamps, and unnamed processes are still running.

We are not broken; we are updating.

It's a work in progress, patching in real time.

I'm going to reboot anyway.

Field Pack for Allies

How to Support the High-Functioning, Quietly Exhausted Person You Love

Some people read this book and see themselves. Others read it and recognize someone they care about, someone composed, competent, and constantly just one project away from a silent, invisible burnout.

This section is for the second group.

Here's What That Wiring Looks Like Up Close

- They'll choose faucet water over fridge water because it saves 15 seconds, and that matters.
- They'll spend hours of mental bandwidth deciding the exact order to do things on Saturday morning.
- They'll avoid apps that make them wait for animations to finish.
- They'll volunteer to run the meeting, then quietly resent being the one who had to.
- They'll reread a brief email six times, imagining how it could be misinterpreted.

None of this is about ego. It's about safety, it's control as protection, and efficiency as morality.

What's Probably True About Them

They're the "strong one." They say "I've got it" even when they're drowning. They've never dropped a ball, but they've quietly resented being the net. They don't melt down; they buffer and then vanish into competence. They look like natural leaders, but their leadership was built, not gifted.

How to Support Them Without Making It Worse

Instead of saying "You're so strong," try "You don't have to carry this alone."

Instead of "Just relax," try "What would make this feel 5% easier today?"

Instead of "You're always so capable," try "When's the last time someone showed up for you?"

Instead of "Let me know if you need anything," try "Here's something I can do. Would that help?"

They don't need coddling. They need permission to not be useful for five minutes.

What Lands Deeper Than You Think

"You don't have to earn rest."

"You don't have to explain why this feels hard."

"I trust you, even when you're not in charge."

"You're allowed to be tired."

"You've carried so much. Can I carry something now?"

They love you with everything they have, but they won't always say "I love you" at the right moment. But they'll memorize your coffee order.

They'll fix the thing you didn't realize was broken. They'll shovel the driveway before you wake up and call it nothing.

They'll try to solve your problems, take on your burdens, and shield you from inconvenience, hassle, or pain.

That's love.

It just doesn't always come with words.

Leadership Code: Patched, Not Deleted

Not everyone is built for leadership.

People like you?

You were wired for it before anyone asked, and long after it stopped being optional.

The problem isn't your instincts. It's the version you downloaded: built for uptime, survival, and systems no one else was willing to fix.

These traits weren't dysfunctional. They were unrefined.

If not me, then who?

Why it stuck: You couldn't unsee what was coming.

Why it hurt: You internalized every system failure you didn't prevent.

The truth: You weren't power-hungry. You were safety-wired.

Reclaim it: Just because you saw the fire doesn't mean you have to run into it alone.

I've got it.

Why it stuck: It meant competence. Safety. Reliability.

Why it hurt: Everyone stopped asking if you were still okay holding it.

The truth: You weren't showing off. You were shielding the system.

Reclaim it: Take command when needed. But don't make competence your cage.

Failure isn't an option.

Why it stuck: You knew what failure felt like and swore you'd never allow it again.

Why it hurt: You stopped allowing yourself to err. No grace. No pause.

The truth: You weren't obsessed with winning. You were trying to keep people from breaking.

Reclaim it: Build systems that fail safely and rebuild faster.

Lead from the front.

Why it stuck: You believed in visible leadership.

Why it hurt: You vanished into execution. No one saw you eroding.

The truth: You weren't just leading. You were the structure.

Reclaim it: Step forward when it counts, but leave space behind you.

Stay calm under pressure.

Why it stuck: You looked composed while others froze.

Why it hurt: You stopped checking in with your own system.

The truth: You **ARE** resilient. You are also overclocked.

Reclaim it: Calm is powerful. So is honesty. Let people see both.

Note for Mental Health Professionals

If you have read this far, thank you.

If you work with someone who thinks the way I do:

• High-functioning,

• Emotionally buffered

• Verbally fluent

You probably already know how difficult it is to move past the surface. They are not resisting you on purpose. They are optimized.

They have been running internal threat assessments longer than they have been in the room. They are practiced at giving just enough to sound reflective while keeping the real system off-limits.

Many people like this seem open and articulate in therapy. They appear self-aware. They offer insight quickly. They speak fluently about patterns, roles, and responsibilities. But they are not emotionally accessible in the ways that matter most.

They are not hiding. They believe they are cooperating. They do not know they are avoiding vulnerability. They believe naming the emotion is the same as feeling it.

I am not a clinician, and this is not a treatment model. It is a firsthand account of what it feels like to live inside a system built for performance, safety, and emotional suppression.

The metaphors in this book:

- Overclocking
- Legacy Code
- Firewall
- Red team
- Patch
- Crash

These are not intended to be clever. They allowed me to name internal processes without shutting down. If someone you are working with seems competent but unreachable, try shifting the language.

Ask what their system was built to protect. Ask what failure simulation is currently running in the background.

This would not have fixed me. But it would have reached me.